FINANCIAL INSTITUTIONS AND SERVICES SERIES

EMERGENCY ECONOMIC STABILIZATION ACT

FINANCIAL INSTITUTIONS AND SERVICES SERIES

Stock Exchanges, IPO's and Mutual funds
E. Klein (Editor)
2004. ISBN: 1-59454-173-6

Global Banking Issues
E. Klein (Editor)
2005. ISBN: 1-59454-172-8

Financial Institutions and Development
E. Klein (Editor)
2005. ISBN: 1-59454-177-9

Capital Formation, Governance and Banking
E. Klein (Editor)
2005. ISBN: 1-59454-191-4

Information Sellers and Resellers
Shane C. Leger (Editor)
2009. ISBN: 978-1-60692-228-6

Hedge Funds: Regulation and Nonregulation
Yeram E. Torrey (Editor)
2009. ISBN: 978-1-60692-041-1

Securitization of Subprime Mortgages
Milton R. Spotgeste (Editor)
2009. ISBN: 978-1-60692-200-2

Reforming Risk in Financial Markets
Melvin R. Turley (Editor)
2009. ISBN: 978-1-60692-445-7

Liquidity, Interest Rates and Banking
Jeffrey Morrey and Alexander Guyton (Editors)
2009. ISBN: 978-1-60692-775-5

U. S. Coins: The Price of a Penny
Walter M. Carvalho (Editor)
2009. ISBN: 978-1-60692-939-1

Econometric Modeling of Value-at-Risk
Timotheos Angelidis and Stavros Degiannakis
2009. ISBN: 978-1-60741-040-9

Global Banking Regulation and Supervision: What are the Issues and What Are the Practices?
James R. Barth, Jie Gan and Daniel E. Nolle
2009. ISBN: 978-1-60741-315-8

Stock Returns: Cyclicity, Prediction and Economic Consequences
George I. Ellison (Editor)
2009. ISBN: 978-1-60741-458-2

Tax Haven Banks
Wade D. Brookins (Editor)
2009. ISBN: 978-1-60692-283-5

Emergency Economic Stabilization Act
Nikola Vazquez (Editor)
2010. ISBN: 978-1-60741-327-1

FINANCIAL INSTITUTIONS AND SERVICES SERIES

EMERGENCY ECONOMIC STABILIZATION ACT

NIKOLA VAZQUEZ
EDITOR

Nova Science Publishers, Inc.
New York

For permission to use material from this book please contact us:
Telephone 631-231-7269; Fax 631-231-8175
Web Site: http://www.novapublishers.com

LIBRARY OF CONGRESS CATALOGING-IN-PUBLICATION DATA

Emergency Economic Stabilization Act / Nikola Vazquez.
p. cm.
Includes index.
ISBN 978-1-60741-327-1 (hardcover)
1. United States. Emergency Economic Stabilization Act of 2008. 2. Banking law--United States. 3. Global Financial Crisis, 2008-2009. I. Vázquez, Nikola.
KF969.582008A2 2009
346.73'082--dc22

2009031686

Published by Nova Science Publishers, Inc. ✦ New York

CONTENTS

PREFACE

Many observers trace the root cause of recent instability in financial markets to uncertainty surrounding the value of widely held securities that are based on mortgages and mortgage-related assets. Losses on these securities have led to the unexpected and relatively sudden failure of several large financial institutions. Credit markets have nearly frozen at times as financial institutions demanded very high interest rates on traditionally routine short-term lending. While there is limited evidence that financial turmoil has caused widespread damage in the broader economy, it is feared that significant real economic effects may be forthcoming, particularly if credit markets remain frozen. This book highlights The Emergency Economic Stabilization Act (EESA), established as law on October 3rd 2008, in response to these economic fears. The Act The Troubled Assets Relief Program (TARP), created by this Act, is also analyzed. Furthermore, the insurance program contained in the enacted version of the EESA is briefly summarized and analyzed. This is an edited, excerpted and augmented edition of various government publications.

Chapter 1 - The Emergency Economic Stabilization Act of 2008 (EESA, Division A of H. R. 1424, P.L. 110-343) provides authority for the Secretary of the Treasury to purchase and insure "troubled assets" to provide stability and prevent disruption in the economy and financial system. The act established two organizations to provide broad oversight for the stability program — a Financial Stability Oversight Board (FSOB) and a Congressional Oversight Panel (COP). The act also placed audit responsibilities for the program with two individuals a new Special Inspector General (IG) for the Troubled Asset Relief Program (TARP), and the Comptroller General (CG) ofthe United States, who heads the Government Accountability Office (GAO). The duties and responsibilities of both oversight panels and both auditors overlap in some areas, but are different in other areas.

Several aspects of the FSOB do not appear to be clearly delineated in the act, including where the FSOB is "established" within the federal government, whether it is covered by a variety of general management laws, and how the FSOB is to be funded and staffed. The act is also unclear regarding certain aspects of the Special IG for the TARP, including where the Office of the Special IG is to be "established" or housed, how or when its authorized appropriation is to be provided, and its specific investigative authorities.

The duties of both oversight panels and both audit organizations overlap in several key areas, and some of the reporting requirements also overlap. Although 18 types of EESA reports are required, none of them specifically require disclosure of how the funds are used by the recipients, and only one is required to be made to the public. The Special IG for the TARP and members of the COP were not named until mid-November 2008. Also, the nature of the "troubled assets" being purchased have changed, perhaps necessitating reassessment of the act's oversight mechanisms. Finally, it is unclear what effect the various oversight and audit mechanisms will have on the balance of power between Congress and the executive branch. Congress gave itself expedited legislative procedures to disapprove actions by the Secretary, but only after the first $350 billion has been obligated.

Several specific requirements in the act appear to contemplate that the "troubled assets" being purchased and insured are primarily residential or commercial mortgages and instruments based on those mortgages. However, recent proposals to deal with the financial crisis are different than these mortgage-based transactions. While the oversight and audit responsibilities of the COP, the FSOB, the CG, and the Special IG still apply, the nature of their specific responsibilities may need to be reconsidered and redefined in light of the type of "troubled assets" that are initially being purchased. It is also unclear how effective all of these oversight and audit requirements will be in ensuring transparency and a balance of power between Congress and the executive branch. This report will be updated when additional information or perspectives become available regarding the act's oversight mechanisms.

Chapter 2 - The current financial instability became widely apparent in the credit markets in August 2007. Although initially thought to be limited to subprime mortgages, increasing defaults on prime mortgages caused losses that rippled through the financial system; the effects have been particularly severe because U.S. mortgage-backed securities (MBS) had previously been viewed as low risk investments. Beginning in early 2008, multiple failures in large financial institutions prompted case-by-case government interventions to address these failures. Dissatisfaction with these ad hoc responses was cited by the Treasury in proposing a broader response focusing on government purchase of troubled mortgage-related assets, hoping to stem uncertainty and fear by removing these assets from the financial system. In early October 2008, Congress passed, and the President signed, the Emergency Economic Stabilization Act of 2008 (EESA, Division A of H.R. 1424/P.L. 110-343), creating the Troubled Assets Relief Program (TARP).

The original three page Treasury proposal focused on purchasing troubled assets from financial institutions. As passed, EESA includes two definitions of troubled assets. The first definition specifies mortgages and mortgage-related assets, including both residential and commercial. The second definition includes any asset that Treasury, in consultation with the Federal Reserve, believes would contribute to financial stability. EESA also includes a troubled asset insurance program to be paid for through premiums. The total amount of assets to be purchased or insured is limited to $700 billion, with a possible congressional resolution of disapproval when the amount exceeds $350 billion. Taxpayers are to be at least partially protected from losses through the provision of equity or debt considerations and through insurance premiums. TARP limits the executive compensation of participating institutions. TARP aims to aid homeowners directly through provisions promoting mortgage restructuring and extending tax relief for homeowners who have mortgage debt forgiven.

On October 14, following enactment of EESA, Treasury announced the creation of a voluntary Capital Purchase Program (CPP). Under this program, up to $250 billion will be injected into financial institutions through government purchases of preferred shares. It is being undertaken under the broad authority provided in the law to make any asset purchases from financial institutions that promote financial stability. In November, the Secretary of the Treasury announced that TARP would focus on capital purchases, although subsequent intervention on behalf of Citibank included support for specific troubled assets.

This report briefly introduces aspects of the current financial instability. Following this, it outlines the EESA legislation and the steps that Treasury has taken to implement EESA. Finally, the report concludes with a more in-depth analysis of the current financial instability, including potential causes of financial instability in general, some sources of the current instability, and how financial instability may spill over into the broader economy. It will be updated as warranted by market and legislative events.

Chapter 3 - The Emergency Economic Stabilization Act of 2008 (EESA, Division A of H.R. 1424, P.L. 110-343) established numerous reporting requirements regarding a variety of issues. The entities charged with preparation of these reports include both new entities established by the act (e.g., the Financial Stability Oversight Board and the Congressional Oversight Panel) as well as agencies and officials who existed before the enactment of EESA (e.g., the Secretary of the Treasury and the Comptroller General of the United States). The recipients of these reports also vary, as well as their timing, frequency, and factors that trigger their development. These differences notwithstanding, all of the EESA reports appear to share a common purpose — to provide information to Congress and other entities on the implementation of the act's provisions.

No single entity receives all of the EESA-required reports. It is not readily apparent why some of the reports are to be filed with a particular set of eight "appropriate committees," some to a subset of those committees, and some to Congress as a whole. Some of the entities designated to prepare or receive the reports have not been formally established (e.g., the Congressional Oversight Panel and the Special Inspector General). Although one of the purposes of the legislation is to provide "public accountability" for the use of EESA authorities, only one of the reports is required to be made to the public, and it is unclear whether the other reports will ultimately be provided to the public. Some of the reports are required to be submitted very quickly, but other reports are not required for years. Some of the reporting requirements are recurring (e.g., every 30 days, or quarterly), while others are one-time requirements. Most of the requirements include clear starting points for the submission of the reports, but in some cases, the starting points are unclear.

Many of the act's reporting requirements seem to address the same or similar issues. The number and variety of the required reports may have been intended to provide a variety of perspectives on the implementation of EESA, but the lack of integration of those requirements may make understanding the implementation of the act difficult. Also, given the nature of the "troubled assets" currently being purchased under the act (i.e., bank stock instead of mortgages or other instruments related to mortgages), it is unclear whether some of the specific requirements are still relevant. Other information that is not specifically required by the act (e.g., how the federal funds are being used by the recipients) may be more helpful to Congress and others as they conduct oversight of the program. Finally, some of the reporting requirements expire on the date that the last troubled asset is sold or transferred, or the date that the last insurance contract expires. Without some kind of a lag period for these requirements, a complete history of the transactions may not be provided.

This report will be updated when new information becomes available.

The Emergency Economic Stabilization Act of 2008 (EESA, Division A of H.R. 1424, which was enacted on October 3, 2008, as P.L. 110-343) established numerous reporting requirements regarding a variety of issues.[1] Some of the reporting requirements are assigned to newly established entities in the act, including the Financial Stability Oversight Board,[2] the Congressional Oversight Panel (COP),[3] and the Special Inspector General for the Troubled Asset Relief Program (SIG TARP).[4] Other reporting requirements are given to agencies and officials who existed before the enactment of EESA (e.g., the Secretary of the Treasury and the Comptroller General of the United States).[5] The recipients of these reports also vary, as well as their timing, frequency, and factors that trigger their development. These differences notwithstanding, all of the EESA reports appear to share a common purpose — to provide information to Congress and other entities on the implementation of the act's provisions.

This report describes the various reporting requirements in EESA and is organized according to the entities required to prepare and submit the reports. The report also provides some concluding observations regarding those requirements. The **Appendix** of the report summarizes the act's reporting requirements in terms of those responsible for producing and receiving the reports, the timing of the reports, and when the reports are scheduled to end.

Chapter 4 - The Emergency Economic Stabilization Act of 2008 (Division A of H.R. 1424, P.L. 110-343) empowers the Secretary of the Treasury to purchase certain "troubled assets" as a means to stabilize the economy. Should the Secretary wish to have more than $350 billion outstanding under the troubled assets program, the President must submit a written report to Congress detailing the Secretary's request and his plan to implement it. The receipt of this report triggers a 15-day period during which Congress may reject the Secretary's request by enacting a joint resolution of disapproval. This disapproval resolution would be considered in the House and Senate under "fast track" parliamentary procedures which are intended to ensure an opportunity to consider and vote on the measure. This report examines these procedures and explains how they differ from the regular parliamentary mechanisms of the House and Senate. It will be updated as needed.[1]

Chapter 5 - Many observers trace the root cause of recent instability in financial markets to uncertainty surrounding the value of widely held securities that are based on mortgages and mortgage-related assets. Losses on these securities have led to the unexpected and relatively sudden failure of several large financial institutions. Credit markets have nearly frozen at times as financial institutions demanded very high interest rates on traditionally routine short-term lending. While there is limited evidence that financial turmoil has caused widespread damage in the broader economy, it is feared that significant real economic effects may be forthcoming, particularly if credit markets remain frozen.

Responding to these economic fears, the House took up the Emergency Economic Stabilization Act of 2008 (EESA) as an amendment to H.R. 3997 on September 29, 2008. This amendment failed by a vote of 205-228. Following this, the Senate took up a bill of the same title with a number of additions and passed it by a vote of 74-25 on October 1, 2008, as an amendment to H.R. 1424. On October 3, 2008, the House passed the amended version of H.R. 1424 by a vote of 263-171. The President signed the bill into law, P.L. 110-343, on the same day. Both versions of the act intend to address recent instability in the financial market through a variety of measures, including an insurance program for "troubled assets." This insurance program would provide U.S. government guarantees for some of the securities that are perceived as being at the root of the current financial instability. This report briefly summarizes and analyzes the insurance program contained in the enacted version of the EESA; it will be updated as warranted by legislative and market events.

Chapter 6 - This report discusses the Special Inspector General provisions in the Emergency Economic Stabilization Act of 2008, H.R. 1424, which was enacted as P .L. 110-343 on October 3, 2008. This Act created a Special Inspector General (SIG) for the Troubled Asset Relief Program (TARP). This report will compare the duties and authorities of the SIG TARP to those of the Special Inspector General for Iraq Reconstruction (SIGIR) and the Special Inspector General for Afghanistan Reconstruction (SIGAR), as well as statutory IGs under the Inspector General Act of 1978, as amended (IG Act).

Congress has established statutory offices of inspectors general (IGs) in many executive and legislative branch agencies, as well as two special IGs for programs and operations funded with amounts appropriated for the reconstruction of Iraq and Afghanistan.[1] The four principal responsibilities of IGs are: (1) conducting and supervising audits and investigations; (2) providing coordination and recommending policies for activities designed to promote economy and efficiency in agency programs and operations; (3) preventing and detecting fraud, waste, and abuse; and (4) keeping the agency head and Congress fully and currently informed about problems and deficiencies relating to such programs and recommending corrective actions.[2] P.L. 110-343 established an additional special IG for the Troubled Asset Relief Program (SIG TARP), which will address the purchase and insurance of troubled assets.

The provisions in P.L. 110-343 establishing the SIG TARP are similar to the IG provisions for SIGIR and SIGAR in many respects. However, there are important substantive distinctions between these three IGs, which this report will refer to collectively as the "special IGs," as well as between the SIG TARP and statutory IGs created under the IG Act.[3] Due to the ambiguous nature of the statutory language in P.L. 110-343, the scope of the powers and authorities of the SIG TARP is not clear, as discussed below.

In: Emergency Economic Stabilization Act ISBN: 978-1-60741-327-1
Editor: Nikola Vazquez

Chapter 1

EMERGENCY ECONOMIC STABILIZATION ACT: PRELIMINARY ANALYSIS OF OVERSIGHT PROVISIONS*

Curtis W. Copeland

SUMMARY

The Emergency Economic Stabilization Act of 2008 (EESA, Division A of H. R. 1424, P.L. 110-343) provides authority for the Secretary of the Treasury to purchase and insure "troubled assets" to provide stability and prevent disruption in the economy and financial system. The act established two organizations to provide broad oversight for the stability program — a Financial Stability Oversight Board (FSOB) and a Congressional Oversight Panel (COP). The act also placed audit responsibilities for the program with two individuals a new Special Inspector General (IG) for the Troubled Asset Relief Program (TARP), and the Comptroller General (CG) ofthe United States, who heads the Government Accountability Office (GAO). The duties and responsibilities of both oversight panels and both auditors overlap in some areas, but are different in other areas.

---

* This is an edited, reformatted and augmented version of a CRS Report for Congress, Report RL34713 dated November 20, 2008.

Several aspects of the FSOB do not appear to be clearly delineated in the act, including where the FSOB is "established" within the federal government, whether it is covered by a variety of general management laws, and how the FSOB is to be funded and staffed. The act is also unclear regarding certain aspects of the Special IG for the TARP, including where the Office of the Special IG is to be "established" or housed, how or when its authorized appropriation is to be provided, and its specific investigative authorities.

The duties of both oversight panels and both audit organizations overlap in several key areas, and some of the reporting requirements also overlap. Although 18 types of EESA reports are required, none of them specifically require disclosure of how the funds are used by the recipients, and only one is required to be made to the public. The Special IG for the TARP and members of the COP were not named until mid-November 2008. Also, the nature of the "troubled assets" being purchased have changed, perhaps necessitating reassessment of the act's oversight mechanisms. Finally, it is unclear what effect the various oversight and audit mechanisms will have on the balance of power between Congress and the executive branch. Congress gave itself expedited legislative procedures to disapprove actions by the Secretary, but only after the first $350 billion has been obligated.

Several specific requirements in the act appear to contemplate that the "troubled assets" being purchased and insured are primarily residential or commercial mortgages and instruments based on those mortgages. However, recent proposals to deal with the financial crisis are different than these mortgage-based transactions. While the oversight and audit responsibilities of the COP, the FSOB, the CG, and the Special IG still apply, the nature of their specific responsibilities may need to be reconsidered and redefined in light of the type of "troubled assets" that are initially being purchased. It is also unclear how effective all of these oversight and audit requirements will be in ensuring transparency and a balance of power between Congress and the executive branch. This report will be updated when additional information or perspectives become available regarding the act's oversight mechanisms.

INTRODUCTION

One of the purposes of the Emergency Economic Stabilization Act of 2008 (EESA, Division A of H.R. 1424, P.L. 110-343) is to "immediately provide authority and facilities that the Secretary of the Treasury can use to restore liquidity and stability to the financial system of the United States."[1] Section 101 of the act ("Purchases of Troubled Assets") authorizes the Secretary of the Treasury to "establish the Troubled Asset Relief Program (or 'TARP') to purchase, and to make and fund commitments to purchase, troubled assets from any financial institution, on such terms and conditions as are determined by the Secretary, and in accordance with this Act and the policies and procedures developed and published by the Secretary." The term "troubled assets" is defined in Section 3(9) of the act as

> (A) residential or commercial mortgages and any securities, obligations, or other instruments that are based on or related to such mortgages, that in each case was originated or issued on or before March 14, 2008, the purchase of which the Secretary determines promotes financial market stability; and (B) any other financial instrument that the Secretary, after consultation with the Chairman of the Board of Governors of the Federal Reserve System, determines the purchase of which is necessary to promote financial market stability, but only upon transmittal of such determination, in writing, to the appropriate committees of Congress.

The act requires the Secretary of the Treasury to implement the program through an Office of Financial Stability within the department's Office of Domestic Finance. The office is to be headed by an Assistant Secretary appointed by the President with the advice and consent of the Senate, although the law permits the Secretary to appoint an interim Assistant Secretary without Senate confirmation.[2]

The Secretary is authorized in Section 101(c) to take "such actions as the Secretary deems necessary to carry out the authorities in this Act." However, Section 101(d) requires the Secretaryto publish program guidelines within two business days after the first purchase of troubled assets.[3] Those guidelines are required to include mechanisms for purchasing troubled assets, methods of pricing and valuing troubled assets, procedures for selecting asset managers, and criteria for identifying troubled assets for purchase. Section 115 of the act initially permits the Secretary to purchase up to $250 billion of troubled assets, and up to a total of $350 billion of assets upon a written certification by the President that the Secretary needs additional authority.[4] Subsequently, if the President submits a written plan to Congress, and if Congress does not object within 15 calendar days (through a joint resolution of disapproval described in subsection 115(c)), the Secretary may purchase up to $700 billion in troubled assets.

Section 102 of the act ("Insurance of Troubled Assets") states that if the Secretary establishes the program authorized in Section 101, then the Secretary "shall establish a program to guarantee troubled assets originated or issued prior to March 14, 2008, including mortgage-backed securities." Specifically, the Secretary is authorized to guarantee the timely payment of up to 100% of the principal and interest related to the assets.

Oversight and Audit Mechanisms

EESA established two organizations to provide broad oversight for the stability program a Financial Stability Oversight Board (FSOB) and a Congressional Oversight Panel (COP). The act also placed audit responsibilities for the program with two individuals — a new Special Inspector General (IG) for the TARP, and with the Comptroller General (CG) of the United States, who heads the Government Accountability Office (GAO).[5] Many ofthe audit and reporting responsibilities delineated in the act specifically reference the actions required in Sections 101 and 102 of the act to purchase troubled assets and to insure those assets.[6]

Questions have been raised by some observers as to whether these oversight and audit responsibilities are complimentary to one another, or are contradictory.[7] This report provides a preliminary comparison and analysis of the specific authorities and responsibilities of the FSOB and the COP, and also compares and analyzes the roles and responsibilities of the Special IG and the CG as described in the act.

The Financial Stability Oversight Board and the Congressional Oversight Panel

As described in EESA, the FSOB and the COP are similar in some respects, but different in other respects. Also, the act is unclear with regard to several key aspects of one or both of these entities. The discussion below and in **Table 1** at the end of this report compares the FSOB and the COP on several relevant dimensions.

Placement Within the Government

The COP is described in Section 125(a) of the act as an "establishment of the legislative branch." In contrast, Section 104(a) of the act simply says that the FSOB is "established," but does not indicate whether the board is part of the executive or legislative branches. All five members of the FSOB are from the executive branch (the Chairman of the Board of Governors of the Federal Reserve System, the Secretary of the Treasury, the Director of the Federal Housing Finance Agency, the Chairman of the Securities and Exchange Commission, and the Secretary of Housing and Urban Development). Therefore, one could reasonably presume that the FSOB is an executive branch entity.

Even if one makes that presumption, however, it is unclear whether the FSOB is intended to be a subunit within the Department of the Treasury or some other agency, or whether the board is intended to be a free-standing, independent entity. The organizational placement of the FSOB may have a number of implications, including whether the board is covered by a variety of statutory management and transparency requirements such as the Federal Records Act, the Federal Advisory Committee Act, the Freedom of Information Act, the Government in the Sunshine Act, and various human resources management and ethics requirements.[8] Legislative branch entities like the COP are generally not subject to these requirements.

Responsibilities

The listed responsibilities of the FSOB (in Section 104(a) of the act) and the COB (in Sections 125(b) and (e) of the act) are similar both in general and with regard to particular elements. For example, both entities are broadly responsible for reviewing the Secretary's actions in carrying out the requirements of the act, and both are specifically responsible for examining the effect of those actions on home ownership, financial markets, and costs to the taxpayers. As discussed in more detail below, both are also required to report to Congress on their findings. However, only the FSOB is charged with (1) making recommendations to the Secretary of the Treasury regarding the use of his authorities under the act; and (2) reporting any suspected fraud, misrepresentation, or malfeasance to the Special IG or the Attorney General of the United States. On the other hand, only the COP is specifically (1) permitted to hold hearings, take testimony, receive evidence, and administer oaths and affirmations to witnesses; and (2) required to report on the extent to which the information on transactions has contributed to market transparency. Also, if so authorized by the panel, any individual member or agent of the COP is authorized to take action on behalf of the panel; no such individualization of authority is permitted by the FSOB.

Access to Information

Section 125(e)(3) of the act authorizes the COP to obtain whatever information it needs to carry out its responsibilities from any federal department or agency, and the heads of those departments or agencies are required to provide the information requested by the chairperson of the panel. As noted previously, the COP is also permitted to take testimony and administer oaths and affirmations to witnesses. The act provides the FSOB no similar right to information from federal departments or agencies, and there does not appear to be any obligation on the part of those departments or agencies to provide that information to the FSOB. Neither the FSOB nor the COP have subpoena authority, and neither is authorized to request the Attorney General to compel agencies to provide needed information.[9]

Membership

As noted previously, Section 104(b) of the act states that the FSOB is comprised of the heads of five executive branch departments or agencies: the Chairman of the Board of Governors of the Federal Reserve System, the Secretary of the Treasury, the Director of the Federal Housing Finance Agency, the Chairman of the Securities and Exchange Commission, and the Secretary of Housing and Urban Development. No provision is made for these agency heads to allow alternates to substitute for them.

Section 125(c) of the act is less directive regarding the members of the COP, merely specifying how members are to be appointed (i.e., one each by the Speaker ofthe House of Representatives, the minority leader ofthe House, the majority leader of the Senate, and the minority leader of the Senate; and one by the Speaker and the majority leader of the Senate, after consultation with the minority leaders in each house). The act does not require that members of the COP be from Congress or even from the legislative branch, but it clearly contemplates Members of Congress as potential members; Section 125(c)(3) specifies that members of the COP who are Members of Congress or full-time officers or employees of the federal government will receive no additional pay, allowances, or benefits. The act does not require that the members of the COP be appointed by a certain date, although (as discussed below) the COP is required to submit its first "regular report" within 30 days after the first exercise of the Secretary's authority under Section 101(a) or 102 of the act, and is required to submit a "special report" on regulatory reform by January 20, 2009.[10] On November 14, 2008, Democratic congressional leaders named the first three members of the panel,[11] and Republican congressional leaders named the remaining two members on November 19, 2008.[12]

Leadership

Section 104(c) of the act specifies that the chairperson of the FSOB is elected by the members of the board, but the act excludes the Secretary of the Treasury from having a vote in that election. According to the interim Assistant Secretary for the Office of Financial Stability, on October 7, 2008, the members of the board selected the Chairman of the Board of Governors of the Federal Reserve System to be chairman of the FSOB.[13] In contrast, although a chairperson of the COP is clearly contemplated by EESA (e.g., Section 125(c)(7) of the act authorizes the chairperson to call meetings), the legislation does not indicate how that chairperson is to be selected.

Pay for Members

The act is silent regarding pay for members of the FSOB, but presumably they would simply receive their regular salaries as the heads of the five agencies. On the other hand, Section 125(c)(2) of the act states that each member of the COP shall be paid at the daily rate of basic pay for level I of the Executive Schedule (the cabinet secretary level, which is $191,300 per year in 2008) for each day that the member is performing duties "vested in the Commission." (The act does not indicate what "commission" is referenced here, but the context suggest that the word "panel" should have been used instead of "commission.") As noted previously, members of the COP who are Members of Congress or full-time federal officers or employees are not allowed to receive additional pay, allowances, or benefits.

Meetings/Quorum

The COP is not required to meet at any specific time; Section 125(c)(7) of the act states that its meetings are held at the call of the chairperson or a majority of its members. However, because the COP is required to submit its first "regular report" within 30 days after the first troubled assets are purchased or insured, meetings of the panel are likely before the report is submitted. Section 125(c)(5) specifies that four members of the COP constitute a quorum, although the act states that a lesser number may hold hearings.

Section 104(d) of the act requires the FSOB to meet two weeks after the first exercise of purchase authority of the Secretary of the Treasury, and monthly thereafter. However, the act does not mention what constitutes a quorum for FSOB action. According to the interim Assistant Secretary for the Office of Financial Stability, the FSOB met on October 7 four days after the legislation was enacted and before the exercise of any purchase authority. In addition to selecting the Chairman of the Federal Reserve to be chairman of the FSOB, the members reportedly adopted the board's bylaws and reviewed the TARP's initial work streams.[14] The FSOB met again on October 13, 2008, and on October 22, 2008.[15] As of mid-November 2008, the FSOB had reportedly met a total of four times, and the minutes of three of those meetings were posted on the Department of the Treasury's website.[16]

Staffing/Consultants

The act does not mention whether and, if so, how the FSOB is to be staffed or paid, and does not indicate whether it can hire experts or consultants. Nevertheless, the interim Assistant Secretary for the Office of Financial Stability testified on October 23, 2008, that the FSOB had appointed staff to the Board, including an executive director, a general counsel, and a secretary.[17]

In contrast, Section 125(d) of the act permits the COP to appoint and fix the pay of "any personnel the Commission considers appropriate." (Again, the context suggests that the word "panel" should have been used instead of "commission.") The COP is also permitted to procure temporary and intermittent experts and consultants for up to one year, and use employees detailed from any federal department or agency. No limits are specified on the number of employees, consultants, or detailees that the COP may obtain, and no limits are specified regarding their pay.

Reports by the Entities

Section 104(g) of the act requires the FSOB to report to the "appropriate committees" of Congress[18] at least quarterly regarding the implementation of its responsibilities, but the act does not specifically indicate when those responsibilities begin. (For example, "quarterly" could mean every three months starting on the date the act was signed into law, or starting on the date that the Secretary of the Treasury begins exercising his authority under the act.) In contrast, Section 125(b)(1) of the act requires the COP to submit a "regular report" of the panel within 30 days after the first exercise of the Secretary's authority under Section 101(a) or 102 of the act, and every 30 days thereafter.[19]

In addition, the COP is required to submit a one-time "special report" by January 20, 2009, analyzing the current regulatory system and its effectiveness at overseeing the participants in the financial system and protecting consumers. The report is also required to contain recommendations for improvement, including whether other participants in the financial markets should be subject to the regulatory system, the rationale for such a recommendation, and whether there are any gaps in existing consumer protections.[20]

Reports to the Entities

The act does not require the FSOB to be the recipient of any reports prepared by other entities, but several provisions in the act specify that certain reports are to be sent to the COP. For example, (1) Section 104(g) of the act requires the FSOB to provide to the COP its quarterly reports to Congress; (2) Section 105(d) states that any report to Congress by the Secretary that is required by Section 105 (e.g., "tranche" reports for each $50 billion of purchases and a "regulatory modernization" report) shall also be provided to the COP; (3) Section 116(d) says that any report or audit required under Section 116 of the act (including Comptroller General reports) shall also be submitted to the COP; (4) Section 117(d) requires the CG's report on "margin authority" to be provided to the COP; (5) Section 121(f)(3) provides that reports by the Special IG for the TARP shall also be submitted to the COP; and (6) Section 129(e) states that the report to certain congressional committees on "exercise of loan authority" shall also be provided to the COP.

Funding

The act does not indicate whether and, if so, how the FSOB is to be funded. In contrast, the act specifies in Section 125(g) that the COP is authorized "such sums as may be necessary for any fiscal year," and specifies that half of the funds are to be derived from the applicable account of the House of Representatives, and half from the contingent fund of the Senate. The act goes on to state in Section 125(h) that an amount equal to the expenses of the COP shall be promptly transferred by the Secretary from time to time upon the presentment of a statement of such expenses by the chairperson of the panel. The funds are to be taken from funds provided to the Secretary under the act and sent to the applicable fund of the House of Representatives and the contingent fund of the Senate.

Termination

Section 104(h) of the act requires that the FSOB and its authority terminate 15 days after (1) the date that the last troubled asset acquired under Section 101 has been sold or transferred out of the ownership of the federal government, or (2) the date of expiration of the last insurance contract under Section 102, whichever is later. Section 125(f) of the act states that the COP is to terminate six months after the authorities provided to the Secretary expire, which is described in Section 120 of the act as December 31, 2009, subject to extension. There are no requirements in the act that either the FSOB or the COP preserve any records, or to provide a means by which the public or others can access any records.

THE SPECIAL INSPECTOR GENERAL FOR THE TARP AND THE COMPTROLLER GENERAL'S ROLE IN THE ACT

As was the case with the two general oversight bodies, the act's descriptions of the duties and responsibilities of the Special IG for the TARP and the Comptroller General are similar in some respects, but differ in other ways. Also, certain elements of the Special IG's operations appear to be undefined. The discussion below and in **Table 2** at the end of this report compares the roles of the Special IG and the CG with regard to several relevant dimensions.

Placement within the Government

Pursuant to the *Bowsher v. Synar* decision of the Supreme Court, it is clear that GAO is a legislative branch agency, and can have no significant executive branch functions.[21] However, although Section 121(a) of EES A "established" the Office of the Special IG for the TARP, the act does not indicate where in the government that office is to be housed. Legislation establishing other special inspectors general, while not specifying organizational placement, contains other indications of where the entity was housed. For example, the Special Inspector General for Iraq Reconstruction was established by Section 3001 of P.L. 108-106, which provided that the IG was appointed by the Secretary of Defense (after consultation with the Secretary of State), and reported to the head of the Coalition Provisional Authority.[22]

The act is also unclear where the Special IG's offices are to be located. Section 116(a)(2)(A) requires the Secretary ofthe Treasury to provide GAO with appropriate audit space and facilities in the Department of the Treasury, but the act contains no similar requirement for the Special IG. However, Section 121(d)(1) of the act says that, in carrying out the duties delineated in the act in subsection (c), "the Special Inspector General shall have the authorities provided in section 6 of the Inspector General Act of 1978." Section 6 of the Inspector General Act (codified at 5 U.S.0 Appendix) states, in relevant part, that the "head of an establishment shall provide the Office within such establishment with appropriate and adequate office space at central and field locations of such establishment, together with such equipment, office supplies, and communications facilities and services as may be necessary." Therefore, if the Special IG is determined to be located within the Department of the Treasury, then the Secretary may be required to provide the Special IG with space and facilities.[23]

Responsibilities

Section 116(a)(1) of the act describes the responsibilities ofthe Comptroller General with regard to the TARP, and Section 121(c)(1) describes the responsibilities ofthe Special IG. The general responsibilities of both the CG and the IG are similar, although stated somewhat differently. For example, once the TARP is established, the CG is to "commence ongoing oversight ofthe activities and performance of the TARP," including the performance of the TARP in meeting the purposes of this Act". The Special IG is to "conduct, supervise, and coordinate audits and investigations of the purchase, management, and sale of assets by the Secretary of the Treasury under any program established under section 101, and the management of the Secretary of any program established under section 102."

The two audit organizations' specific responsibilities are similar, but also differ in some ways. For example, while both the CG and the Special IG are required to identify the troubled assets acquired under the program, only the Special IG is charged with describing why the Secretary deemed it necessary to purchase each asset, and to list (with detailed biographical information) each person or entity hired to manage the troubled assets. The CG, on the other hand, is the only entity specifically required to examine the internal controls of the TARP, to examine the efficiency of TARP operations and contracting procedures, and to review the TARP's efforts to minimize conflicts of interest.

The act gives two responsibilities to the CG that are not given to the Special IG. Section 116(b)(1) of the act requires the CG to audit the TARP's financial statements, and Section 117 requires the CG to determine the extent to which leverage and sudden deleveraging of financial institutions was a factor behind the financial crisis, including the roles of the Board of Governors of the Federal Reserve System, the Securities and Exchange Commission, the Secretary of the Treasury, and others.

When Audits Begin

Section 121(b)(1) requires the President to nominate the Special IG "as soon as practicable after the establishment of any program under sections 101 and 102." According to an interim final rule issued by the Board of Governors of the Federal Reserve System, on October 14, 2008, the Secretary of the Treasury announced a program within the TARP to provide capital to eligible financial institutions.[24] Therefore, it appears that a "program" triggering the nomination of the Special IG has been established. The interim Assistant Secretary for the Office of Financial Stability said that Treasury officials were "working with the White House to identify candidates for possible nomination and confirmation in November."[25] Also, Section 121(e) of the act indicates that the Office of the Special IG is to be provided $50 million from the proceeds of the sale of securities, including Treasury bills and savings bonds.[26] However, the act does not indicate when or how those funds are to be provided, so it is unclear when the Office of the Special IG will be operational.

The act says that the CG's audit functions are to begin "upon establishment of the troubled asset relief program." According to the interim Assistant Secretary and the acting CG, GAO has already begun its reviews. GAO officials and staff met with Treasury officials on October 9, and they reviewed certain contracts on October 12.[27] At least one Member of Congress has expressed support for these actions by GAO.[28]

Access to Information

The act provides both the CG and the Special IG with access to certain information, although those rights differ somewhat.[29] Section 116(a)(2)(B) states that, consistent with applicable law, the CG has access to any information or "things" belonging to the TARP, and to its officers, employees, or agents. Section 121(e)(4) requires the heads of other agencies to furnish the Special IG with any requested information or assistance that is "practicable" and not in contravention to law. Therefore, the CG appears to have specific access rights to information from the TARP, whereas the Special IG appears to have specific access only to information from other agencies. Also, the act requires that the CG be given "full facilities for verifying transactions with the balances or securities held by depositaries, fiscal agents, and custodians," and is permitted to make and retain copies of any records. No similar rights are specifically afforded the Special IG.

As noted previously, however, Section 121(d)(1) of the act says that, in carrying out the duties delineated in the act in subsection (c), "the Special Inspector General shall have the authorities provided in section 6 of the Inspector General Act of 1978." Section 6 of the Inspector General Act states, in relevant part, that each inspector general is authorized to "have access to all records, reports, audits, reviews, documents, papers, recommendations, or other material available to the applicable establishment which relate to programs and operations with respect to which that Inspector General has responsibilities under this Act." That section goes on to authorize the IGs to require by enforceable subpoena the production of all information, documents, and other evidence needed in the performance of the functions assigned by the act.

Obligation of the TARP to Respond to Audits

Section 116(b)(3) of the act requires the TARP to address deficiencies that the CG identifies, or to certify to the appropriate committees of Congress that no action is needed. The act places no similar requirement on the TARP regarding audit findings by the Special IG.

Staffing/Contracting

Section 121(e) of the act permits the Special IG to select, appoint, and employ as many officers and employees as he or she deems necessary, but the selection, classification, and pay of those employees is governed by the requirements of current civil service law in Title 5, *United States Code.* That section also permits the Special IG to employ experts and consultants at a rate not to exceed GS-15 of the General Schedule (the top end of which is currently $149,000 per year in Washington, D.C.), and to enter into contracts for other audits or studies. These authorities are similar to those provided to other statutory inspectors general under the Inspector General Act of 1978. The act contains no similar provisions for the CG, but GAO already has similar abilities under its existing statutory authorities.[30]

Reports

Both the CG and the Special IG are required to submit reports regarding their audit activities to the appropriate committees of Congress, but some of the specifics are unclear and appear to be different. For example, Section 116(a)(3) requires the CG to submit GAO's reports at least every 60 days, but does not specifically indicate when the first 60-day period begins. Section 121(f)(1) requires the Special IG's reports to include a "detailed statement of all purchases, obligations, expenditures, and revenues associated with any program established by the Secretary of the Treasury under sections 101 and 102." In contrast, the CG is simply required to submit reports of "findings under this section." The CG is required to submit GAO's reports to the Special IG, among others; the Special IG is not required to reciprocate, but is required (by Section 121(f)(3) of the act) to submit its reports to the COP. Notably, in contrast to reports from statutory inspectors general, neither the CG's reports nor the Special IG's reports are sent to the Secretary of the Treasury or any other executive branch official. It is also unclear whether the Department of the Treasury will be allowed to comment on GAO's or the Special IG's findings before the reports are sent to Congress, or whether the reports are to be made public.

Funding

Section 116(a)(2)(C) of the act requires the Department of the Treasury to reimburse GAO for the full cost of any oversight activities that are billed by the CG. Section 116(b)(1) requires the department to reimburse GAO for the full cost of the audit of the TARP financial statement — a requirement that is similar to one in the Government Accountability Office Act of 2008 (P.L. 110-323).[31]

In contrast, Section 121(g) of the act requires that $50 million of the funds from the proceeds of the sale of securities under Section 118 be provided to the Special IG to carry out his or her responsibilities. Section 118 of the act states that the Secretary "may use the proceeds of the sale of any securities issued under chapter 31 of title 31, United States Code" for the authorities granted in the act and the cost of administering those authorities. Chapter 31 of title 31 ("Public Debt") includes Treasury bills, savings bonds and savings certificates, and other instruments. However, the timing and mechanics of the transfer of funds to the Special IG are unclear (e.g., whether the Special IG gets a one-time payment of $50 million at the time the office is established, or whether that amount is to be provided over a longer period of time, as determined by the Secretary of the Treasury).

Termination

Section 121(h) of the act specifies that the Office of the Special IG terminates on the later of (1) the date the at the last troubled asset acquired under Section 101 has been sold or transferred, or (2) the date of expiration of the last insurance contract under Section 102.[32] Section 116(e) says that the CG's oversight, audit, and reporting requirements under the act also terminate on those dates. Also, Section 116(a)(2)(A) states that the Secretary of the Treasury is to provide the CG with audit space and facilities until the termination date specified in Section 120 (which is December 31, 2009, subject to extension). There are no requirements in the act that either the CG or the Special IG preserve any records or provide a means by which the public or others can access any records.

Concluding Observations

The Secretary of the Treasury's initial proposal to purchase troubled assets was very short and contained no oversight provisions. Instead, it stated that, "Decisions by the Secretary pursuant to the authority of this Act are non-reviewable and committed to agency discretion, and may not be reviewed by any court of law or any administrative agency."[33] Several Members of Congress and many others, including both of the major party presidential candidates, called for increased oversight of the program. For example, Senator John McCain said, "We won't solve a problem caused by poor oversight with a plan that has no oversight."[34]

In contrast, as enacted on October 3, 2008, EESA contained an elaborate oversight system, with general oversight responsibilities given to the FSOB and the COP, and with detailed auditing responsibilities assigned to the Comptroller General and a new Special Inspector General for the TARP. Other, albeit more limited, responsibilities were assigned to OMB, CBO, and the Joint Committee on Taxation to help Congress oversee the implementation of the TARP. Together, 11 different entities are required to prepare and submit a total of 18 different types of reports to six different entities, with many of those reports required to be submitted on a recurring basis.[35] No single entity receives all of the reports.

Overlapping Responsibilities

The duties and responsibilities of both oversight panels and both audit organizations overlap in several key areas. For example, both the FSOB and the COP are broadly required to review how the Secretary of the Treasury uses the act's authorities. Likewise, the Special IG and the CG have similar general responsibilities (e.g., to "oversee the activities and performance of the TARP" and to audit the "purchase, management, and sale of assets under any Section 101 program"), as well as similar specific responsibilities.[36] Even where the entities' responsibilities differ, it is not clear why certain responsibilities were given to one organization instead of another.

Some of the EESA reporting requirements also appear to overlap, even for the same entity. For example, Section 105(a) of the act requires the Secretary of the Treasury to report to the "appropriate committees" within 60 days after the first use of his authority in Sections 101 and 102, and every 30 days afterward, on all "actions taken by the Secretary," including all agreements, transactions, and insurance contracts. Section 105(b) requires the Secretary to report to the same committees on the same transactions within seven days of each $50 billion in commitments to purchase troubled assets. Section 116 requires the Comptroller General to oversee the activities of the TARP and report on his findings at least every 60 days, which would presumably include TARP-related agreements, transactions, and insurance contracts. Section 121 requires the Special Inspector General to report every quarter on his audits of (among other things) all "troubled assets" purchased or sold under Section 101, and the management of any insurance program under Section 102.

Congress may have wanted these overlaps and divisions of responsibility to occur, providing it with differing perspectives on the same issues. However, in practice, the areas of overlap may prove to be counterproductive, particularly if the bodies are not sharing relevant information and, as a result, are reaching different conclusions based on incomplete or variable data and methods. Also, with duplicative and uncoordinated oversight, the Secretary of the Treasury and other officials responsible for implementing the financial rescue plan may spend the bulk of their time responding to requests for information from multiple entities asking the same questions. One author commented that, once it was clear that some type of oversight was needed in EESA, "consensus seemed to have been reached by including everyone's favorite idea in the bill, with no one thinking hard about how all of them fit together and whether more oversight is necessarily better than less.[37]

Possible Additions to Reporting Requirements

These numerous oversight and audit requirements notwithstanding, it is unclear how effective they will be in ensuring that the underlying purpose of the TARP is being met, or that the program is transparent to the public. None of the reports are specifically required to address one of the central issues that have been raised about the purchases of these troubled assets — how the funds provided by the Secretary of the Treasury are being used by the recipients of those funds. Initially, the Secretary of the Treasury indicated that troubled assets would be purchased to increase lending by the banks.[38] He later said that he decided to purchase stock in financial institutions instead of bad assets because buying those assets would take too long to recapitalize the banks for lending.[39] However, a number of questions have been raised by Members of Congress and others about whether the banks that received the initial $115 billion were using the money to pay dividends to stockholders, to pay bonuses to corporate executives, or to finance the purchases of smaller banks — not to increase lending.[40]

Although none of these activities are prohibited uses of the funds, it is notable that none of the reports specifically require the disclosure of how the money is being used. Senator Richard Shelby was quoted as saying that "We don't know who's benefitting from this, [or] where the money's going."[41] The nominee to be the Special Inspector General for the TARP reportedly said he believes that he has the statutory authority needed to determine how the banks spent the money,[42] but he is not specifically required to include that information in his reports.

Also, only one of the 18 types of EESA reports is required to be made to the public.[43] All of the other reports are required to be submitted to Congress, the "appropriate" committees of Congress, or to one of the oversight or auditing bodies. While either the preparers or the recipients of these reports may be able to make them public, they are not required to do so.[44] Concerns have been raised about a perceived lack of transparency in various aspects of the financial system rescue program, including the contracts that have been awarded, and the securities being accepted as collateral for loans to the banks.[45]

A Delayed Start for the COP and the Special IG

Although the FSOB and GAO began their oversight and auditing responsibilities quickly, as of mid- November 2008 more than six weeks after EESA was enacted the COP and the Special IG have not been fully established. The act requires the leadership in the House and the Senate to select the five members of the COP. On November 14, 2008, the first three members of the panel were named,[46] and the final two members were named on November 19.[47] As of the date of this report, however, the panel had not met or hired staff, and a substantial portion of the $700 billion in funds had already been committed to purchase bank stock and other "troubled assets."

Also, the COP was required to submit its first "regular report" within 30 days of the Secretary's first purchase of "troubled assets." Because the first purchase of bank stock occurred on October 28, the first report may be required before, or shortly after, the COP is fully established. Also, the COP is required to submit its "special report" by January 20, 2009, "analyzing the regulatory system and its effectiveness at overseeing the participants in the financial system," and making recommendations for reform. It is unclear whether the COP can conduct this ambitious study and produce a report of this magnitude in such a short period of time.

EESA required the President to nominate the Special IG for the TARP "as soon as practicable after the establishment of any program under sections 101 and 102." Although the Secretary of the Treasury announced the establishment of such a program on October 14, 2008, the President did not nominate a Special IG until one month later, on November 14, 2008.[48] The Senate Committee on Banking, Housing, and Urban Affairs held a confirmation hearing on the nomination for November 19, 2008, and the nomination could be acted upon by the full Senate shortly thereafter.[49] EESA requires the first report by the Special IG to be submitted within 60 days after confirmation. Also, the act states that the Special IG is to be provided $50 million from the proceeds of the sale of securities to carry out the act's requirements, but it is unclear when those payments are to be made and in what amounts. At a hearing before the Senate Finance Committee on November 17, 2008, the Special Inspector General nominee said he was unsure whether $50 million would be enough to fund the office's operations.[50]

In the absence of the Special IG, the inspector general for the Department of the Treasury, Eric M. Thorson, has been attempting to oversee the implementation of EESA in addition to his regular responsibilities. He reportedly has "a few dozen" people working on the program part time, but has said that the new office should have at least 100 full time employees.[51] It is also unclear whether the Treasury IG can carry out responsibilities that Congress has specifically assigned to the Special IG. On November 13, 2008, the Treasury IG was quoted as saying, "It's a mess," and "I don't think anyone understands right now how we're going to do proper oversight of this thing."[52]

Possible Reassessment of Oversight Mechanisms

Some of the oversight and auditing requirements may need to be reassessed given the changed nature of the TARP. When EESA was enacted on October 3, 2008, the type of "troubled assets" that were generally expected to be purchased under the TARP were those fitting the first definition in Section 3(9) of the act —i.e., "residential or commercial mortgages and any securities, obligations, or other instruments that are based on or related to such mortgages."[53] The composition of some of the oversight bodies, and the specific oversight and auditing responsibilities given to those entities, appear to have been predicated on this expectation.[54]

However, on October 14, 2008 — less than two weeks after EESA was enacted the Secretary of the Treasury announced that initial funds authorized by the act would be used to purchase preferred shares of stock in certain banks.[55] Congress had authorized the Secretary to take such action when it defined a "troubled asset" in Section 3(9) of EESA as both mortgage-based financial instruments as well as "any other financial instrument that the Secretary ... determines the purchase of which is necessary to promote financial stability." Subsequent developments seemed to confirm this shift in direction. On October 25, 2008, the *Washington Post* reported that the Department of the Treasury was "dramatically expanding the scope of its bailout of the financial system with a plan to take ownership stakes in the nation's insurance companies."[56] Treasury officials were also reportedly in discussions about using TARP or other funds to address liquidity problems facing state and local governments.[57] as well as U.S. automakers.[58]

Then, on November 12, 2008, the Secretary of the Treasury announced that the department no longer planned to buy troubled mortgage-based assets from financial firms, but would instead provide "aid to banks and other firms that issue student, auto and credit card loans in part by jump starting the market that provides financing for these companies."[59] Firms that reportedly could be eligible for this new round of capital purchases include insurers and specialty lenders for small businesses. The Secretary said that the department had decided that buying mortgage-based assets would take too long to recapitalize the financial institutions, and that buying equity in these firms would be a more powerful incentive for them to lend.[60]

While the oversight and audit responsibilities of the COP, the FSOB, the CG, and the Special IG may still generally apply to these new TARP-related programs, the makeup and the nature of their specific responsibilities may need to be reconsidered and redefined in light of the type of "troubled assets" being purchased and the other types of programs being considered. For example, given the current focus on purchasing bank stock instead of mortgage-based securities, members of the FSOB could be appointed based on their expertise in the banking industry (e.g., the head of the Federal Deposit Insurance Corporation or the Comptroller of the Currency) in addition to, or instead of, those appointed to the board based on their housing-related expertise. Similarly, congressional leaders have been encouraged to include state representation on the COP, in recognition of the importance financial institutions have on state economies.[61]

In addition, to the extent that the Secretary establishes programs based on statutory authorities outside of Sections 101 and 102 of EESA, the audit responsibilities of both the CG and the Special IG may need to be redefined to ensure that they cover all aspects of the program. For example, Section 116(a)(1) defines the CG's "scope of oversight" as "the activities and performance of the TARP and of any agents and representatives of the TARP (as related to the agent or representative's activities on behalf of or under the authority of the TARP), including vehicles established by the Secretary under this Act." Section 3(8) of the act defines the TARP as "the Troubled Asset Relief Program established under section 101." Similarly, Section 121(c) of the act defines the duties of the Special IG as audits and investigations of the "purchase, management, and sale of assets by the Secretary of the Treasury under any program established by the Secretary under section 101, and the management by the Secretary of any program established under section 102." Since all of these audit functions are geared to Sections 101 and 102 of the act, it is unclear whether the CG or the Special IG can audit or investigate programs established pursuant to other sections of the act (e.g., the proposed program to guarantee troubled mortgages under Section 109).[62] However, during Senate hearings on his nomination to be Special IG for the TARP, several Senators reportedly told Neil M. Barofsky that he should assume that he has authority for all aspects of EESA.[63]

Certain Issues Are Unclear

The information provided in the body of this report also suggests that certain aspects of these oversight and auditing organizations may need to be clarified. For example, it is currently unclear where the FSOB is located within the federal government, or whether it is covered by a variety of general management and transparency requirements. Also, unlike the COP, the act does not provide the FSOB with a statutory right to information from federal departments or agencies. When the FSOB meets, it is not clear whether all or a majority of members must be present to take action, as the act does not specify what constitutes a quorum. The act does not indicate whether, and if so how, the FSOB is to be funded or staffed, or whether it can employ consultants to help it carry out its mission. As a result, it may be difficult for the board to carry out some of the tasks that it has been assigned (e.g., reporting evidence of fraud or malfeasance) particularly since several members of the FSOB are likely to change at the end of this Administration. Although the FSOB is required to report "quarterly," the act does not specify when those quarterly periods begin. The FSOB also does not appear to receive any of the various reports that are provided to the COP (e.g., reports by the Special IG or the CG).

In addition, although the act states that the Office of the Special IG is "established," it does not indicate where the office will be housed, and (in contrast to the provisions regarding GAO) there is no specific requirement in the act that the Secretary of the Treasury or any other department or agency provide the office with space or facilities. (However, if the Office of the Special IG is considered part of the Department of the Treasury, then the Secretary may be required by the Inspector General Act of 1978 to do so.) Finally, the act indicates that both the Office of the Special IG and GAO's audit and reporting responsibilities under the act terminate on the date that the last asset is sold or the last insurance contract expires, whichever is later. It is therefore unlikely that reports of the Special IG will reflect all relevant transactions, as some period after those dates will likely be needed to summarize the information and provide a complete historical record. GAO's final report, however, could address those transactions under the CG's general authority in 31 LT. S .C. §§712 and 717.[64]

Table 1. Characteristics of the Financial Stability Oversight Board and the Congressional Oversight Panel in the Emergency Economic Stabilization Act of 2008

	Financial Stability Oversight Board (FSOB) (Section 104)	Congressional Oversight Panel (COP) (Section 125)
Placement Within the Federal Government	Unclear. Subsection (a) simply says the FSOB is "established".	(a) An "establishment of the legislative branch."
Responsi-bilities	(a) The FSOB is responsible for — (1) reviewing the exercise of authority under a program developed in accordance with this Act, including — (A) policies implemented by the Secretary and the Office of Financial Stability created under Sections 101 and 102, including the appointment of financial agents, the designation of asset classes to be purchased, and plans for the structure of vehicles used to purchase troubled assets; and — (B) the effect of such actions in assisting American families in preserving home ownership, stabilizing financial markets, and protecting taxpayers; (2) making recommendations, as appropriate, to the Secretary regarding use of	(b) The COP shall review the current state of the financial markets and the regulatory system, and submit "regular reports" to Congress on — (1) the use by the Secretary of authority under the act, including the use of contracting authority and the administration of the program; (2) the impact of purchases made under the act on financial markets and financial institutions; (3) the extent to which information made available on transactions has contributed to market transparency; and (4) the effectiveness of foreclosure mitigation efforts and the effectiveness of the program from the standpoint of minimizing long-term costs to the taxpayers and maximizing the benefits for taxpayers.

Table 1. (Continued)

	Financial Stability Oversight Board (FSOB) (Section 104)	Congressional Oversight Panel (COP) (Section 125)
	the authority under this Act; and (3) reporting any suspected fraud, misrepresentation, or malfeasance to the Special Inspector General for the Troubled Assets Relief Program or the Attorney General of the United States, consistent with Section 535(b) of title 28, United States Code.	
Other Authorities and Powers	(e) In addition to the above responsibilities, the FSOB has the authority to ensure that the policies implemented by the Secretary are — (1)in accordance with the purposes of the Act; (2) in the economic interests of the United States; and (3) consistent with protecting taxpayers, in accordance with Section 113(a) (entitled "Minimization of Long-Term Costs and Maximization of Benefits for Taxpayers")	(e)(1) In carrying out its responsibilities, the COP may hold hearings, "sit and act at times and places," take testimony, receive evidence, and administer oaths and affirmations to witnesses. (e)(2) Any member or agent of the COP may, if authorized by the panel, take any action which the COP is authorized to take.
Access to Data	No mention.	
Membership	(e)(3) The COP may secure directly from any department or agency of	

Table 1. (Continued)

	Financial Stability Oversight Board (FSOB) (Section 104)	**Congressional Oversight Panel (COP) (Section 125)**
	the U.S. information needed to carry out its responsibilities. Upon request of the chairperson of the COP, the head of any department or agency shall furnish such information.	
Leadership	(c) The COP shall consist of five members, with one member each appointed by (1) the Speaker of the House of Representatives; (2) the minority leader of the House of Representatives; (3) the majority leader of the Senate; (4) the minority leader of the Senate; and (5) the Speaker and the majority leader of the Senate, after consultation with the minority leaders of each house. (c)(6) A vacancy on the COP shall be filled in the same manner as the original appointment.	Although Section (c)(7) authorizes a "chairperson" of the COP to call meetings, the act does not indicate how the chairperson is selected.
Pay for Members	No mention	(c)(2) Each member of the COP shall be paid at the daily rate of basic pay for level I of the Executive Schedule ($191,300 in 2008) for each day the member is performing duties in the Commission (3) However, members of the COP who are Members of Congress or full-time federal officers or employees of the

Table 1. (Continued)

	Financial Stability Oversight Board (FSOB) (Section 104)	Congressional Oversight Panel (COP) (Section 125)
		U.S. receive no additional pay, allowances, or benefits.
Meetings	(d) The FSOB shall meet two weeks after the first exercise of purchase authority of the Secretary and monthly thereafter.	(c)(7) The COP shall meet at the call of the chairperson or a majority of its members.
Quorum	No mention.	(c)(5) Four members of the COP constitute a quorum, but a lesser number may hold hearings.
Subordinate Bodies	(f) The FSOB may appoint a credit review committee to evaluate the use of the purchase authority provided under the Act and the assets acquired through the use of that authority.	No mention.
Staffing and Consultants	No mention	(d)(1) The COP may appoint and fix the pay of any personnel it deems appropriate. (d)(2) The COP may procure temporary and intermittent services under Section 3109(b) of title 5 (experts and consultants for up to one year). (d)(3) Upon request of the COP, the head of any federal department or agency may detail (on a reimbursable basis) any personnel of that department or agency to the COP.

Table 1. (Continued)

	Financial Stability Oversight Board (FSOB) (Section 104)	Congressional Oversight Panel (COP) (Section 125)
Reports by the Entity	(g) The FSOB shall report to the appropriate committees of Congress and the COP not less than quarterly regarding its responsibilities under subsection (a).	(b)(1)(B) The "regular reports" of the COP (described in subsection (a) above) shall be submitted within 30 days after the first exercise of the Secretary's authority under Section 101(a) or 102, and every 30 days thereafter. (b)(2) The COP is also to submit a "special report on regulatory reform" not later than Jan. 20, 2009, analyzing the current regulatory system and its effectiveness at overseeing the participants in the financial system and protecting consumers, with recommendations for improvement (including whether other participants in the financial markets should be subject to the regulatory system, the rationale for such a recommendation, and whether there are any gaps in existing consumer protections).
Reports to the Entity	No mention.	Per Section 104(g) of the act, the FSOB is to provide its quarterly reports to Congress to the COP. Per Section 105(d), any report to Congress by the Secretary that is required by section 105 shall also be provided to the COP. Per Section 116(d), any report

Table 1. (Continued)

	Financial Stability Oversight Board (FSOB) (Section 104)	**Congressional Oversight Panel (COP) (Section 125)**
		or audit required under section 116 of the act (including Comptroller General reports) shall also be submitted to the COP. Per Section 117(d), the Comptroller General's report on "margin authority" is also to be provided to the COP. Per Section 121(f)(3), reports by the Special Inspector General for the TARP shall also be submitted to the COP. Per Section 129(e), the report to certain congressional committees on "exercise of loan authority" shall also be provided to the COP.
Funding	No mention.	(g)There is authorized to be appropriated to the COP such sums as may be necessary for any fiscal year, half of which shall be derived from the applicable account of the House of Representatives, and half from the contingent fund of the Senate. (h) An amount equal to the expenses of the COP shall be promptly transferred by the Secretary from time to time upon the presentment of a statement of such expenses by the chairperson of the panel. The funds are to be taken from funds provided to the Secretary under the act and sent to the applicable fund of

Table 1. (Continued)

	Financial Stability Oversight Board (FSOB) (Section 104)	**Congressional Oversight Panel (COP) (Section 125)**
		the House of Repres-entatives and the contingent fund of the Senate.
Termination	(h) The FSOB and its authority shall terminate 15 days after the later of (1) the date that the last troubled asset acquired under Section 101 has been sold or transferred out of the ownership of the federal government, or (2) the date of expiration of the last insurance contract under Section 102.	The COP shall terminate 6 months after the termination date in Section 120 (Dec. 31, 2009, subject to extension)

Oversight and the Balance of Power

It is unclear what effect the various oversight and audit mechanisms will have on the balance of power between Congress and the executive branch. EESA gave the Secretary of the Treasury broad authority to purchase "troubled assets," and defined that term to include any financial instrument that the Secretary deems "necessary to promote financial market stability." Congress gave itself expedited legislative procedures to disapprove actions by the Secretary, but only after the first $350 billion has been obligated.[65] Congress can use its regular legislative procedures to disapprove actions regarding the first $350 billion of asset purchases, but a presidential veto of any congressional action (whether through regular or expedited procedures) would require a two-thirds vote of both houses of Congress to prevent the Secretary's actions from taking effect. Also, legislation has been introduced in the 110th Congress to reverse the presumption and require Congress to *approve* any expenditure over $350 billion,[66] but the President could veto this type of initiative as well—again requiring a two- thirds majority in both houses of Congress for enactment.

Table 2. Responsibilities of the Comptroller General and the Special Inspector General for the TARP in the Emergency Economic Stabilization Act of 2008

	Comptroller General (CG) (Section 116)	Special Inspector General (IG) (Section 121)
Placement Within the Federal Government	GAO is a legislative branch agency (per *Bowsher v. Syncr,* 478 U.S. 714, at 734 (1986)).	Unclear, although presumably within the Department of the Treasury (since the Secretary is authorized to establish the TARP).
Responsi-bilities	(a) (1) The CG shall oversee the activities and perfor-mance of the TARP and its agents and representatives, including: —(A) the performance of the TARP in meeting the purposes of the Act, particularly foreclosure mitigation, cost reduction, stability of financial markets or banking system, and protection of taxpayers; —(B) the financial condition and internal controls of the TARP and its agents; —(C) the characteristics of transactions and commitments entered into, including type, frequence, size, prices paid, terms/conditions, and terms of future commitments; —(D) the characteristics and disposition of acquired assets, including type, acquisition price, market value, sale prices and terms, and use of proceeds);	(c) (1) The Special IG shall conduct, supervise, and coordinate audits and investigations of the purchase, management, and sale of assets under any Section 101 program, and the management of any program under Section 102, including by collecting and summarizing: —(A) a description of the categories of troubled assets purchased or procured by the Secretary; —(B) a listing of the troubled assets in each category; —(C) an explanation of why the Secretary deemed it necessary to purchase each asset; —(D) a listing of each institution selling those assets; —(E) a listing (with detailed biographical information) of each person or entity hired to manage such troubled assets; —(F) a current estimate of the amount of troubled assets on the books, purchased, and sold, and the profit or loss on each sale; and

Table 2. (Continued)

	Comptroller General (CG) (Section 116)	**Special Inspector General (IG) (Section 121)**
	—(E) the efficiency of TARP operations in using appropriated funds; —(F) the compliance of TARP and its agents with applicable laws and regulations; —(G) TARP's efforts to prevent, identify, and minimize conflicts of interest by its agents; — (H) the efficiency of contracting procedures pursuant to Section 107(b) (minority and women contracting). (b)(2) The CG may audit the programs/activities of the TARP, its agents, and any vehicles established.	— (G) a listing of the insurance contracts issued. (c)(3) In addition to the above, the Special IG shall also have the authorities provided to IGs in section 6 of the Inspector General Act of 1978.
Obligation to Respond to Its Audits	(b)(3) The TARP is required to take action to address defici-encies identified by the CG or other auditor engaged by the TARP, or to certify to the appropriate committees of Congress that no action is needed.	No specific provision (although the Inspector General Act requires agencies to furnish requested information or assistance).
Audit Space and Facilities	(a)(2)(A) The Secretary shall provide appropriate audit space and facilities in the Department of the Treasury.	No specific provision (although the Inspector General Act requires agencies to furnish office space and facilities).
Staffing and Contracting	No provision (although GAO will likely use existing staff and contracting authority)	(e) The Special IG may (1) select, appoint, and employ such officers and employees as may be necessary, subject to the provisions of title 5

Table 2. (Continued)

	Comptroller General (CG) (Section 116)	Special Inspector General (IG) (Section 121)
		regarding appointments, classification, and pay; (2) employ experts and consultants at daily rates not to exceed GS-15; and (3) enter into contracts or other arrangements for audits and studies as may be necessary.
Access to Data and Records	(a)(2)(B) To the extent consistent with law, the CG has access to any information, data, reports, papers, or things belonging to or used by the TARP, and to officers, agents, advisors, and employees. The CG shall be given full facilities for verifying transactions, and may make and retain copies of any records.	(e)(4) Upon request of the IG, the head of other agencies shall furnish any requested information or assistance that is practicable and not in contrav-ention of law. If information or assistance is unreasonably refused, the IG shall report to the appropriate committees of Congress without delay.
Appointment, Removal, and Pay of the Auditor	N/A	(b)(1) The Special IG is to be appointed by the President, with the advice and consent of the Senate. (2) The appointment is to be made on the basis of integrity and demonstrated ability in accounting, auditing, financial analysis, law, management analysis, public administration, or investigation. (3) The nomination is to be made as soon as practicable after the establishment of any program under Sections 101 and 102. (4) The IG may be removed by the President, with communication of the reason to Congress. (6) The

Table 2. (Continued)

	Comptroller General (CG) (Section 116)	**Special Inspector General (IG) (Section 121)**
		IG shall be paid the same as other presidentially-appointed IGs.
Reports	(a)(3) The CG shall submit reports of findings to the appropriate committees of Congress and to the Special IG for the TARP at least every 60 days. The CG may also submit special reports as warranted by GAO's findings. (b)(1) The CG is to annually audit the TARP's financial statements. Also, Section 117 requires the CG to determine the extent to which leverage and sudden deleveraging of financial institutions was a factor behind the crisis, including the roles of the Board of Governors, the SEC, the Secretary, and others.	(f)(1) The Special IG shall submit a report to the appropriate committees of Congress summarizing the IG's activities during the relevant period within 60 days after confirmation and each calendar quarter thereafter. Each report shall include a detailed statement of all purchases, obligations, expenditures, and revenues associated with any program under Sections 101 and 102, as well as information under subsection (c)(1). (f)(2) None of the above authorizes the disclosure of information that is prohi-bited from disclosure by law or exe-cutive order, or part of a criminal investigation. (f)(3) The reports shall also be submitted to the COP.
Funding	(a)(2)(C) Treasury shall reimburse GAO for the full cost of any oversight activities as billed by the CG. (b)(1) Treasury is also to reimburse GAO for the full cost of the audit of the TARP financial statement. In both cases, the reimbursements are credited to GAO's "salaries and expenses"	(g) Of the funds available to the Secretary of the Treasury under Section 118 (from the sale of securities), $50 million shall be provided to the Special IG until expended.

Table 2. (Continued)

	Comptroller General (CG) (Section 116)	**Special Inspector General (IG) (Section 121)**
	appropriation account and available until expended.	
Termination	(e) Any oversight, reporting, or audit requirement termin-ates on the later of (1) the date that the last troubled asset acquired under Section 101 has been sold or transferred or (2) the date of expiration of the last insurance contract under Section 102. (a)(2) Secretary is to provide the CG with space and facilities until the termination date in Section 120 (Dec. 31, 2009, subject to extension).	(h)The Office of the Special IG shall terminate on the later of (1) the date that the last troubled asset acquired under Section 101 has been sold or transferred or (2) the date of expiration of the last insurance contract under Section 102.

Senate confirmation of agency officials is another means by which Congress can provide oversight of executive branch actions, and that authority will be particularly relevant regarding the nomination of the Assistant Secretary of the Treasury for the Office of Financial Stability. However, the legislation permits the Secretary of the Treasury to appoint an interim Assistant Secretary, and places no limit on how long that appointee may serve. Given the scope of the Assistant Secretary's responsibilities and the need for immediate action, a nomination for the position may not be submitted during the remaining days of the 110th Congress. The only other position established by EESA that requires Senate confirmation is the Special Inspector General for the TARP. As noted previously, the Senate Committee on Banking, Housing, and Urban Affairs held a confirmation hearing on the nomination for November 19, 2008, and the nomination could be acted upon by the full Senate shortly thereafter.[67]

End Notes

[1] For more information on EESA and related issues, see CRS Report RL34730, *The Emergency Economic StabilizationAct and Current Financial Turmoil: Issues and Analysis,* by Baird Webel and Edward V. Murphy.

[2] On October 6, 2008, the Secretary of the Treasury named Assistant Secretary Neel Kashkari as interim Assistant Secretary for the Office of Financial Stability.

[3] On October 28, 2008, the Department of the Treasury transferred the first EESA-related funds to participating institutions. See the remarks of Under Secretary for Domestic Finance Anthony Ryan at [http ://www treasury.gov/pres s/releas es/hp 1240. htm] . The department has also published guidelines for the TARP Capital Purchase Program and a list of frequently asked questions. See [http://www.treas.gov/press/releases/hp1222.htm] for a copy of those documents.

[4] The President has certified to Congress that the additional $100 billion will be needed. See [http ://www.whitehouse. gov/news/releas es/2008/ 10/20081014-1 .html] for a copy of the President's certification.

[5] GAO's responsibilities in the act are in addition to its existing responsibilities. For example, 31 U.S.C. §712(1) requires the CG to "investigate all matters related to the receipt, disbursement, and use of public money," and 31 U.S.C. §717(b) states that the CG shall "evaluate the results of a program or activity the Government carries out under existing law." For more information on GAO, see CRS Report RL30349, *GAO: Government Accountability Office and General Accounting Office,* by Frederick M. Kaiser.

[6] The act also requires certain reports from the Office of Management and Budget (OMB) and the Congressional Budget Office (CBO). For example, Section 202(a) requires OMB to report to the President and the Congress within 60 days of the first exercise of authority under Section 101(a) (or by December 31, 2008, whichever comes earlier), and semiannually thereafter on how much the troubled asset program is costing, how that cost estimate was derived, and how the estimate changed from the previous report. CBO is required to assess the OMB reports within 45 days of their submission to the Congress. Also, Section 201 of the act authorizes CBO and the Joint Committee on Taxation to receive "all information used by the Secretary in connection with activities authorized under this Act" to assist Congress with its oversight responsibilities.

[7] See, for example, Gibson, Dunn & Crutcher LLP, "Financial Markets in Crisis: Section-by-Section Analysis of the Emergency Economic Stabilization Act of 2008," available at [http ://blogs law.harvard. edu/corpgov/files /2008/ 10/100208-analysis-economics abilizati onact08.pdf]. The authors note that the oversight entities "overlap considerably," and that while Congress may want multiple perspectives, "the potential for these oversight entities to trip over each other in the course of their work is great."

[8] See, for example, CRS Report RL32592, *General Management Laws and the 9/11 Commission's Proposed Office of National Intelligence Director (NID) and National Counterterrorism Center (NCTC)*, coordinated by Clinton T. Brass and Curtis W. Copeland. That report indicated that more general management laws would appear to cover the MD and NCTC if they were independent entities in the executive branch than if they were placed within the Executive Office of the President. If the FSOB is considered part of a federal department or agency or an independent agency, then most of these general management laws would appear to apply. For more information about these management statutes, see CRS Report RL30795, *GeneralManagement Laws : A Compendium*, coordinated by Clinton T. Brass.

[9] In contrast, the legislation establishing the Privacy and Civil Liberties Oversight Board (121 Stat. 355) authorizes the Board to request the Attorney General to subpoena information on its behalf.

[10] As noted earlier in this report, the Department of the Treasury transferred the first EESArelated funds to participating institutions on October 28, 2008.

[11] Amit R. Paley, "N.Y. Prosecutor Picked to Oversee Bailout," *Washington Post,* November 15, 2008, p. Dl. Democratic congressional leaders reportedly selected Richard H. Neiman, superintendent of banks in New York; Elizabeth Warren, a professor at Harvard Law School; and Damon Silvers, associate general counsel of the AFL-CIO.

[12] Amit R. Paley, "Senators Moving Quickly to Install Bailout Watchdog," *Washington Post,* November 20, 2008, p. A10. Those named were Senator Judd Gregg and Representative Jeb Hensarling.

[13] See interim Assistant Secretary Kashkari's remarks before the Institute of International Bankers, at [http://www.cnbc.com/id/27160443].

[14] Ibid. See [http://www.treasury.govinitiatives/eesa/docs/AmendedBylaws.pdf] for a copy of the bylaws.

[15] Testimony ofNeel Kashkari, interim Assistant Secretary for the Financial Stability Office, U.S. Department of the Treasury, before the Senate Committee on Banking, Housing, and Urban Affairs, October 23, 2008.

[16] See [http://www.treas.govinitiatives/eesa/minutes.shtml] to view those minutes.

[17] Testimony ofNeel Kashkari, interim Assistant Secretary for the Financial Stability Office, U.S. Department of the Treasury, before the Senate Committee on Banking, Housing, and Urban Affairs, October 23, 2008.

[18] Section 3(1) of the act defines the term "appropriate committees of Congress" as the Committee on Banking, Housing, and Urban Affairs, the Committee on Finance, the Committee on the Budget, and the Committee on Appropriations of the Senate; and the Committee on Financial Services, the Committee on Ways and Means, the Committee on the Budget, and the Committee on Appropriations of the House of Representatives.

[19] As noted earlier in this report, the Department of the Treasury transferred the first EES A-related funds to participating institutions on October 28, 2008.

[20] S. 3652, introduced by Senator Maria Cantwell on September 29, 2008, would have established an independent, bipartisan commission to conduct a similar review of the U.S. financial system. The bill also would have established a special inspector general for financial markets oversight.

[21] *Bowsher v. Synar,* 478 U.S. 714, at 734 (1986).

[22] For a detailed comparison of the Special IG for the TARP and other special IGs as well as statutory IGs under the Inspector General Act of 1978, as amended, see CRS Report RS22981, *The Special Inspector General for the Troubled Asset Relief Program (SIG TARP),* by Vanessa K. Burrows.

[23] According to the interim Assistant Secretary for the Office of Financial Stability, in anticipation of the upcoming nomination and confirmation of the Special IG, the Department of the Treasury has already begun meeting with the department's IG.

[24] See U.S. Department of the Treasury, "Tarp Capital Purchase Program; Interim Final Rule," 73 *Federal Register* 62205, October 20, 2008, for a copy of this rule.

[25] See interim Assistant Secretary Kashkari's remarks before the Institute of International Bankers, at [http : //www. cnbc. com/id/27160443 .

[26] Specifically, Section 121(g) of the act says that "Of the amounts made available to the Secretary of the Treasury under section 118, $50,000,000 shall be available to the Special Inspector General to carry out this section." Section 118 states that the "Secretary may use the proceeds of the sale of any securities issued under chapter 31 of title 31, United States Code." Chapter 31 of Title 31 ('Public Debt") includes savings bonds and savings certificates (Section 3105), retirement and savings bonds (Section 3106), and other vehicles.

[27] See interim Assistant Secretary Kashkari's remarks before the Institute of International Bankers, at [http : //www. cnbc. com/id/27160443 .

[28] Humberto Sanchez, "Frank Praises GAO for Oversight of Treasury Rescue Plan," *Congress Daily,* October 14, 2008.

[29] GAO has certain data access rights under existing law. For example, 31 U.S.C. §716(a) states that each agency is to "give the Comptroller General information the Comptroller General requires about the duties, powers, activities, organization, and financial transactions of the agency."

[30] For example, 31 U.S.C. §731 permits the Comptroller General to procure the services of up to 20 experts and consultants for up to three years at daily rates of pay for level IV of the Executive Schedule (currently $149,000 per year).

[31] Section 6 of that legislation provides that, after October 1, 2009, if GAO "audits any financial statement or related schedule which is prepared under section 3515 by an executive agency," the agency must reimburse GAO for the cost of the audit if GAO audited the statement for FY2007.

[32] In comparison, the posts of Special Inspector General for Iraq Reconstruction and Special Inspector General for Afghanistan Reconstruction are each to end 180 days after its parent entity's reconstruction funds are less than $250 million.

[33] Andrew Ross Sorkin, "A Bailout Above the Law," *New York Times,* September 23, 2008, P. Cl.

[34] Michael Cooper and Patrick Healey, "McCain, More Critical of Bailout Plan, Faults Oversight," *New York Times,* September 22, 2008, available at [http://www.nytimes.com/2008/09/23/us/politics/23campaign.html].

[35] For a complete listing of the reports required by EESA, see CRS Report RL34740, *Reporting Requirements in the Emergency Economic Stabilization Act of 2008,* by Curtis W. Copeland.

[36] For example, the CG is to describe the "characteristics and disposition of acquired assets." The Special IG is to provide a "description of the categories of troubled assets purchased or procured by the Secretary," and a "listing of the troubled assets in each category."

[37] Alan Morrison, "Plugging Leaks in the Bailout,"*Legal Times,* November 10, 2008, p. 46.

[38] For example, in his statement upon the passage of EESA, the Secretary of the Treasury said that the authority provided in the act "gives us the ability to protect and recapitalize our financial system as we work through the stresses in our credit markets." To view a copy of this statement, see [http://www.treasury.gov/press/releases/hp1175.htm].

[39] Aaron Lorenzo and R. Christian Bruce, "Treasury Pulls Back From TARP Purchase of Mortgage-Related Assets, Paulson Says,"*BNA Daily Report for Executives,* November 13, 2008, p. AA-1.

[40] See, for example, Mark Landler, "New Terrain for Arbiters of a Bailout," *New York Times,* November 4, 2008, p. B1, which said "critics from Capitol Hill to Wall Street are lashing out at the program, saying the banks are misusing the capital infusions by hoarding the money rather than lending it, as the Treasury Secretary, Henry M. Paulson Jr., urged in order to unclog the credit markets.... Critics also say that, by not barring banks from paying dividends or hefty bonuses, the Treasury is leading taxpayers to think that their money is being spent frivolously." Also, see Binyamin Appelbaum, `Banks to Continue Paying Dividends; Bailout Money is for Lending, Critics Say," *Washington Post,* October 30, 2008, p. Al; and Charlene Carter, "Leading House Democrats Pressure Treasury on Banks' Use of Federal Funds," *Congress Now,* October 31, 2008, available at [http ://congres snow. gallerywatch. com/ArticleDetail.aspx? articleID= 7182] .

[41] R. Christian Bruce, "Federal Overseer Will Seek Real-Time Data From TARP Asset Mangers and Contractors," *BNA Daily Report for Executives,* November 20, 2008, p. A-20.

[42] Terry Kivian, "Special IG Nominee Pledges Enforcement of TARP Rules," *Congress Daily PM,* November 19, 2008, available at [http ://www.nationalj ournal. com/congres s daily/ cdp 20081119 5781.php?related=true&storyl=null&story2=null&story3=null].

[43] Section 116(b) of the act requires TARP to prepare and issue audited financial statements to the appropriate committees of Congress and the public.

[44] For example, the Department of the Treasury posted the first "tranche" report on its public website even though EESA did not require the report to be provided to the public. To view a copy, see [http://www.treas.gov/initiatives/eesa/docs/Tranche-Reportfinal.pdf].

[45] See, for example, Ben Protess, "Bailout Does Still Redacted,"*ProPublica,* November 13, 2008, available at [http ://www.propublica.org/article/bailout-docs-still-redacted-1113%20/]; and Dean Starkman, "Bloomberg Steps Up; Wire Service Sues Fed for Bailout Transparency," *Columbia Journalism Review,* November 7, 2008, available at [http://www.cjr.org/the_audiebloomberg_steps_up.php].

[46] Amit R. Paley, "N.Y. Prosecutor Picked to Oversee Bailout," *Washington Post,* November 15, 2008, p. Dl. Democratic congressional leaders reportedly selected Richard H. Neiman, superintendent of banks in New York; Elizabeth Warren, a professor at Harvard Law School; and Damon Silvers, associate general counsel of the AFL-CIO.

[47] Amit R. Paley, "Senators Moving Quickly to Install Bailout Watchdog," *Washington Post,* November 20, 2008, p. A10. Republican congressional leaders selected Senator Judd Gregg and Representative Jeb Hensarling.

[48] Mike Soraghan, `Bush Picks a Bailout Watchdog," *The Hill,* November 14, 2008. The nominee is Neil M. Barofsky, of New York.

[49] Pursuant to Senate rules, the Senate Homeland Security and Governmental Affairs Committee has the right to hold a hearing on inspectors general, or else 20 days must pass before the nomination proceeds to the full Senate. However, the nomination could be brought to the full Senate by unanimous consent.

[50] R. Christian Bruce and Ralph Lindeman, "Drawdown of Remaining TARP Funds May Be Left for Obama Administration,"BNA *Daily Report for Executives,* p. A-23.

[51] Amit R. Paley, "Bailout Lacks Oversight Despite Billions Pledged," *Washington Post,* November 13, 2008, p. Al.

[52] Ibid.

[53] For example, the legislation was described as having "granted authority to purchase up to $700 billion in troubled mortgage-backed securities from debt-riddled Wall Street firms, a move designed to free up the credit markets." Michael Kranish and Jenny Paul, "Resounding Yes to Bailout," *Boston Globe,* October 4, 2008, p. Al.

[54] For example, several members of the FSOB appear to have been named to the board because of their relationship to the housing industry (e.g., the Director of the Federal Housing Finance Agency and the Secretary of Housing and Urban Development). Section 116(a)(1) of the act states that the CG is to describe the "characteristics of transactions and commitments entered into, including transaction type, frequency, size, prices paid, and all other relevant terms and conditions, and the timing, duration and terms of any future commitments to purchase assets." The CG is also required to describe the "characteristics and disposition of acquired assets, including type, acquisition price, current market value, sale prices and terms, and use of proceeds from sales."

[55] David Cho, Neil Irwin, and Peter Whoriskey, "US Forces Nine Major Banks to Accept Partial Nationalization," *Washington Post,* October 14, 2008, p. A-1; and Neil Irwin and David Cho, "Paulson's Change in Rescue Tactics," *Washington Post,* October 15, 2008, p. D-1.

[56] David Cho, Binyamin Appelbaum, and Zachary A. Goldfarb, "Bailout Expands to Insurers," *Washington Post,* October 25, 2008, p. Al.

[57] Yin Wilczek, "MSRB in Discussions Concerning Possible Bailout of State, Local Governments," *BNA Daily Report for Executives,* October 28, 2008, p. A-21.

[58] Nora Macaluso, "Federal Aid Crucial for Survival of U.S. Automakers, Analysts Say," *BNA Daily Report for Executives,* October 30, 2008, p. AA-1.

[59] Peter Whoriskey, David Cho, and Binyamin Appelbaum, "Treasury Redefines Its Rescue Program; Plan to Buy Distressed Assets is Abandoned in Favor of Aid to Loosen Consumer Credit," *Washington Post,* November 13, 2008, p. Al.

[60] Aaron Lorenzo and R. Christian Bruce, "Treasury Pulls Back From TARP Purchase of Mortgage-Related Assets, Paulson Says," *BNA Daily Report for Executives,* November 13, 2008, p. AA-1.

[61] Stephen Joyce, "New York Governor Pushes for State Representation on TARP Oversight Panel," *BNA Daily Report for Executives,* October 28, 2008, p. A-28.

[62] On October 23, 2008, the interim Assistant Secretary for the Office of Financial Stability testified before the Senate Committee on Banking, Housing, and Urban Affairs that the department was considering implementing a large-scale program to guarantee troubled mortgages, which is authorized under Section 109 of EESA.

[63] Amit R. Paley, "Senators Moving Quickly to Install Bailout Watchdog," *Washington Post,* November 20, 2008, p. A10. Senators Claire McCaskill and Charles E. Grassley reportedly introduced legislation on November 19, 2008, to make clear that the Special IG has authority over all aspects of EESA, and to allow him to hire staff without following the civil service hiring process.

[64] As noted earlier in this report, 31 U. S.C. 712(1) requires the CG to "investigate all matters related to the receipt, disbursement, and use of public money," and 31 U.S.C. §717(b) states that the CG shall "evaluate the results of a program or activity the Government carries out under existing law."

[65] As noted earlier in this report, Section 115(a)(3) of the act states that if the President sends Congress a written report describing the Secretary of the Treasury's plan to spend the second $350 billion, Congress has 15 calendar days to enact a joint resolution of disapproval. For more information about this process, see CRS Report RS22985, *"Fast Track" Parliamentary Procedures of the Emergency Economic Stabilization Act,* by Christopher M. Davis. Although no written report has been submitted, legislation has already been introduced in the 110th Congress (H. J.Res . 101) to invoke this requirement (i.e., to prevent expenditures above $350 billion).

[66] See, for example, S. 3683, S. 3694, S. 3697, and H.R. 7276 in the 110th Congress.

[67] Pursuant to Senate rules, the Senate Homeland Security and Governmental Affairs Committee has the right to hold a hearing on inspectors general, or else 20 days must pass before the nomination proceeds to the full Senate. However, the nomination could be brought to the full Senate by unanimous consent.

In: Emergency Economic Stabilization Act
Editor: Nikola Vazquez
ISBN: 978-1-60741-327-1

Chapter 2

THE EMERGENCY ECONOMIC STABILIZATION ACT AND CURRENT FINANCIAL TURMOIL: ISSUES AND ANALYSIS*

Baird Webel and Edward V. Murphy

SUMMARY

The current financial instability became widely apparent in the credit markets in August 2007. Although initially thought to be limited to subprime mortgages, increasing defaults on prime mortgages caused losses that rippled through the financial system; the effects have been particularly severe because U.S. mortgage-backed securities (MBS) had previously been viewed as low risk investments. Beginning in early 2008, multiple failures in large financial institutions prompted case-by-case government interventions to address these failures. Dissatisfaction with these ad hoc responses was cited by the Treasury in proposing a broader response focusing on government purchase of troubled mortgage-related assets, hoping to stem uncertainty and fear by removing these assets from the financial system. In early October 2008, Congress passed, and the President signed, the Emergency Economic Stabilization Act

---

* This is an edited, reformatted and augmented version of a CRS Report for Congress, Report RL34730 updated November 25, 2008.

of 2008 (EESA, Division A of H.R. 1424/P.L. 110-343), creating the Troubled Assets Relief Program (TARP).

The original three page Treasury proposal focused on purchasing troubled assets from financial institutions. As passed, EESA includes two definitions of troubled assets. The first definition specifies mortgages and mortgage-related assets, including both residential and commercial. The second definition includes any asset that Treasury, in consultation with the Federal Reserve, believes would contribute to financial stability. EESA also includes a troubled asset insurance program to be paid for through premiums. The total amount of assets to be purchased or insured is limited to $700 billion, with a possible congressional resolution of disapproval when the amount exceeds $350 billion. Taxpayers are to be at least partially protected from losses through the provision of equity or debt considerations and through insurance premiums. TARP limits the executive compensation of participating institutions. TARP aims to aid homeowners directly through provisions promoting mortgage restructuring and extending tax relief for homeowners who have mortgage debt forgiven.

On October 14, following enactment of EESA, Treasury announced the creation of a voluntary Capital Purchase Program (CPP). Under this program, up to $250 billion will be injected into financial institutions through government purchases of preferred shares. It is being undertaken under the broad authority provided in the law to make any asset purchases from financial institutions that promote financial stability. In November, the Secretary of the Treasury announced that TARP would focus on capital purchases, although subsequent intervention on behalf of Citibank included support for specific troubled assets.

This report briefly introduces aspects of the current financial instability. Following this, it outlines the EESA legislation and the steps that Treasury has taken to implement EESA. Finally, the report concludes with a more in-depth analysis of the current financial instability, including potential causes of financial instability in general, some sources of the current instability, and how financial instability may spill over into the broader economy. It will be updated as warranted by market and legislative events.

INTRODUCTION

The Emergency Economic Stabilization Act (EESA)[1] became law on October 3, 2008. Intended to restore stability to the U.S. financial system, the act created a Troubled Assets Relief Program (TARP).[2] TARP included two primary programs: a troubled asset purchase program and a troubled asset insurance program. This report briefly introduces characteristics of current financial instability. It also outlines the EESA legislation and the steps that Treasury has taken to implement EESA. Next, the report provides an in-depth analysis of financial instability, including potential causes of instability in general, and how it may spill over into the broader economy. Finally, the report assesses the causes of this period of financial instability. This report will be updated as warranted by market and legislative events.

Starting in the 1980s, non-bank lenders have originated increasing shares of U.S. mortgages. These non-bank lenders obtained their own funds through the conversion of mortgages into marketable securities (securitization), rather than by accepting consumer deposits as in the traditional banking model.[3] In most cases, once a mortgage was made, the entity that originated the loan sold it to another institution, which then pooled a large number of these loans together. From this pool of loans, the institution then issued securities whose returns were based on the payments made on the underlying mortgages in the pool. For a variety of market and regulatory reasons, these mortgage-backed securities (MBS) became widely held by most financial institutions in the United States and by many institutions worldwide. In addition to the securities directly backed by mortgages, financial institutions created numerous other complex securities and derivatives based on the initial MBS. These secondary products, such as collateralized debt obligations (CDO) and credit default swaps (CDS) were also very widely held.

In 2006 and 2007, the rates of default and non-payment by mortgage holders increased significantly. This, in turn, ultimately caused the securities and derivatives based on these mortgages to lose value. In some cases, securities thought to be low risk were completely wiped out. These losses have rippled through the financial system, causing problems for institutions in a number of unexpected ways as well as stress to the general financial system. The failures of large financial institutions, including Bear Stearns, IndyMac, Fannie Mae, Freddie Mac, Lehman Brothers, and AIG, were part of this turmoil.[4] Due largely to the uncertainty about what future mortgage default rates will be, what institutions are exposed to mortgage-related assets, and whether more institutions may fail unexpectedly, financial markets have nearly frozen at various points in time since August 2007.

Difficulties for individual financial institutions, and for financial systems as a whole, can often usefully be distinguished as problems of liquidity or of capital adequacy.[5] A firm suffering from liquidity problems has assets whose values significantly outweigh liabilities, but is unable to liquidate these assets fast enough to meet short-term obligations. A firm suffering from capital adequacy problems has an inadequate buffer between its assets and its liabilities; if its asset values fall or liability values rise unexpectedly, the firm may be unable to meet its liabilities even if its assets can be liquidated quickly. Insolvency could result. The classical prescription for addressing liquidity problems is for a lender of last resort (such as the Federal Reserve) to lend freely, but at high enough interest rates so that institutions do not take too many risks. Capital adequacy problems, particularly when widespread, can be more difficult to address. In past crises, steps have included directly bolstering firms' capital[6] and sweeping insolvent, or near insolvent, firms out of the system.[7]

THE TROUBLED ASSETS RELIEF PROGRAM

Executive and Congressional Proposals

On September 19, 2008, the Secretary of the Treasury proposed a broad program of financial intervention to stabilize markets. The Treasury plan called for government purchases of up to $700 billion in mortgage-related securities, in the hope that, by partially purging the system of these troubled assets, normal functioning of the financial markets could be restored.

The idea of broad asset purchases, as in the original Treasury plan, is only one of a number of methods that could be used to address the uncertainties regarding mortgage-related assets. Among the other concepts put forward have been

- a federal guarantee program to insure mortgage-related assets, thus eliminating much of the uncertainty surrounding these securities;
- direct capital injections by the Treasury into financial institutions, thus shoring up their capitalization; and

direct support for homeowners, thus decreasing mortgage default rates and increasing the value of mortgage-related securities.

After various legislative proposals and drafts were circulated and negotiations between Congress and the administration were conducted, the Emergency Economic Stabilization Act of 2008 (EESA), was brought to a vote in the House as substitute amendment to H.R. 3997; this amendment failed in the House on a vote of 205-228 on September 29, 2008. Another version of EESA, which included the original EESA plus several other provisions not in the first bill,[8] was offered on October 1 in the Senate as an amendment (S.Amdt. 5685) to an unrelated bill, H.R. 1424, which had previously passed the House. The amendment to H.R. 1424 was approved by a Senate vote of 74-25; it was then taken up by the House and passed by a vote of 263-171 on October 3, 2008. The President signed the amended version of H.R. 1424, now P.L. 110-343, the same day as House passage.

Provisions of TARP as Enacted

Asset Purchase Program

Section 101 of EESA provides authority to the Secretary of the Treasury to purchase "troubled assets" from any financial institution established and regulated under federal or state law, but excluding any foreign governmental entity. These assets are defined by the statute as "residential or commercial mortgages," including securities "based on, or related to such mortgages." In addition to the mortgage-related assets that were the focus of the program, the Secretary is authorized to purchase "any other financial instrument" that is "necessary to promote financial market stability." Congress must be notified of the Secretary's determination to purchase non-mortgage related assets, but the Secretary does not need Congress' approval to do so. The Secretary is to take steps to prevent "unjust enrichment" of financial institutions selling assets to the government, in particular preventing the sale of troubled assets at a price higher than what the seller initially paid for the asset. Section 113 directs the Secretary to use market mechanisms, such as auctions, to purchase assets when possible.

Asset Insurance Program[9]

Section 102 of EESA provides that, if the asset purchase program is created, the Secretary must also create an insurance program providing federal guarantees for troubled assets. This insurance program is to be funded by premiums paid by financial institutions for the federal guarantee, with no specific provision for the TARP insurance fund to borrow from the U.S. Treasury. Under the statute, the guarantees may be up to 100% of the value of the asset and the premiums may be risk-based, but the Secretary is not required to implement either of these provisions.

Size of the Programs

Under Sections 115 and 102, the total size of the insurance and asset purchase program combined is not to exceed $700 billion at any given time, which does allow the program to buy and sell assets, then use the sales proceeds to purchase other assets. Authority to purchase or insure $250 billion is effective on the date of enactment, with an additional $100 billion in authority effective upon submission of a Presidential certification. The final $350 billion in authority may be exercised upon transmission of a written report by the President detailing the plan for the exercise of this authority. Congress has 15 calendar days to pass a joint resolution under "fast track" rules, to deny the authority to use the final $350 billion.[10]

Private Equity and Debt Considerations

Section 113 requires that, in return for federal purchase of troubled assets, financial institutions must provide to the federal government either debt or equity considerations, such as preferred or common stock in that institution. These considerations are to provide protection for the taxpayer against losses on troubled asset sales and allow the taxpayers to benefit from future equity appreciation of institutions participating in TARP.

Oversight Provisions[11]

The EESA creates a number of oversight mechanisms. Section 104 establishes a Financial Stability Oversight Board to oversee the authorities in the act. Section 105 requires detailed monthly reports by the Secretary to Congress on the operations of the program. Section 116 gives the Comptroller General oversight and audit authority on TARP, including access to records and office space within the Treasury for employees of the Government Accountability Office (GAO) to exercise this oversight. Should GAO identify problems in the annual audit, TARP must either take action to correct the problems, or certify to Congress that no action is necessary. Section 121 creates a Special Inspector General to oversee TARP, who shall report quarterly to Congress. Section 125 creates a Congressional Oversight Panel made up of five congressional appointees.

Assistance to Homeowners

One of the specific considerations Section 103 requires be taken into account in the general operation of TARP is "to help families keep their homes." EESA also includes specific measures to that end. Section 109 directs the Secretary, as TARP acquires mortgages and mortgage-related securities, to encourage servicers to take advantage of the HOPE for Homeowners Program.[12] The Secretary is also required to consent to reasonable requests for loan modifications from homeowners whose loans are acquired by the government. Section 110 requires the Federal Housing Finance Agency, the Federal Deposit Insurance Corporation, and the Federal Reserve Board to implement a plan to "maximize assistance for homeowners," including reduction of interest rates or reduction of loan principal, for mortgages or mortgage backed securities owned or managed by these institutions.

Section 303 extends an additional exception to the tax laws, first made available by the Mortgage Forgiveness Debt Relief Act of 2007,[13] relating to the cancellation of mortgage debt. The additional exception allows for the exclusion of discharged qualified residential debt from gross income. Qualified indebtedness is defined as debt, limited to $2 million ($1 million if married filing separately), incurred in acquiring, constructing, or substantially improving the taxpayer's principal residence that is secured by such residence. It also includes refinancing of this debt, to the extent that the refinancing does not exceed the amount of refinanced indebtedness. The taxpayer is required to reduce the basis in the principal residence by the amount of the excluded income. The provision does not apply if the discharge was on account of services performed for the lender or any other factor not directly related to a decline in the residence's value or to the taxpayer's financial condition. The provision applies to debt discharges that are made on or after January 1, 2007, and before January 1, 2013.[14]

Executive Compensation

Sections 111 and 302 put limits on executive compensation for firms participating in TARP. For institutions whose assets are bought directly,

Section 111 requires that the Secretary publish standards that will (1) limit incentives for executives to take excessive risks, (2) provide for recovery of any bonus paid based on earnings statements that later prove to be inaccurate, and (3) prohibit golden parachute payments to senior executives. These standards are to be in effect for the duration of time that the government holds an equity or debt interest in the company. For those institutions whose assets are bought at auction, only new employment contracts with "golden parachutes" are prohibited.

Section 302 provides special tax rules pertaining to executive compensation for participants in TARP. In particular, Section 162(m) of the Internal Revenue Code is amended to reduce the limitation on deductible executive compensation from $1,000,000 to $500,000 and Section 280G of the Internal Revenue Code is amended to expand the definition of a parachute payment for covered employees of TARP participants.

Mark-to-Market Accounting

Sections 132 and 133 address "mark-tomarket" accounting rules required under Statement 157 of the Financial Accounting Standards Board (FASB). The Securities and Exchange Commission (SEC) is specifically given the authority to waive these accounting rules. In addition, the SEC is directed to conduct an expansive study on mark-to-market accounting and what impact it may have had on the current financial turmoil.

Increase in Deposit Insurance

Section 135 provides for a temporary increase in the insurance on deposits in federally insured banks and credit unions.[15] From enactment until the end of 2009, this amount is increased from $100,000 to $250,000. This temporary increase may not be taken into account when setting premiums for deposit insurance.

Assistance to Financial Institutions Holding Fannie Mae/Freddie Mac Preferred Stock

Section 301 provides tax relief to financial institutions holding preferred stock in Fannie Mae or Freddie Mac, which lost significant value after the government conservatorship announced in September 2008. Capital gains or losses from the sale or exchange of preferred stock of Fannie Mae and Freddie Mac will be treated as ordinary income or loss by applicable financial institutions, which include banks, mutual savings banks, cooperative banks, and savings and loan associations, among others. The basic rationale behind this tax relief is that it will reduce the need of the bank "to obtain additional capital from the FDIC or investors. This should also prevent some community banks from becoming insolvent."[16] Normally, in the case of corporations, capital losses are allowed only to the extent of capital gains, although the losses may be carried back three years or carried forward for five years. This provision allows these financial institutions to use the losses incurred in the government takeover of Fannie Mae and Freddie Mac to reduce their tax liability this year (a year with few capital gains), rather than carry the losses to past tax years or forward to future tax years.[17]

Duration of Program

Section 120 authorizes TARP asset purchases until the end of 2009. Upon receipt of certification and supporting information from the Secretary, this termination date may be extended until October 3, 2010 (two years after the date of enactment).

Treasury Actions since Enactment

Although the original discussion of the three-page draft Treasury plan focused on removing bad assets from financial institution balance sheets, some policymakers urged, and H.R. 1424/P.L. 110-343 included, broad discretion for the use of TARP funds. The potential scope of the program can be found in Part (B) of the definition of a troubled asset, which includes

> ... any other financial instrument that the Secretary, after consultation with the Chairman of the Board of Governors of the Federal Reserve System, determines the purchase of which is necessary to promote financial market stability, but only upon transmittal of such determination, in writing, to the appropriate committees of Congress.

Shortly after passage, Treasury announced its plans to implement the program, which will be coordinated by Neel Kashkari, the Interim Assistant Secretary for the Office of Financial Stability. Mr. Kashkari created teams within Treasury to administer TARP, including hiring asset managers to administer asset purchases, proposing rules for asset insurance, injecting capital into banks through preferred stock purchases, and announcing a homeowner assistance program. Although Treasury has subsequently announced that it will focus on capital purchases, the following section describes the various programs authorized by TARP.[18]

Asset Purchase

Treasury must fulfill certain logistical and statutory conditions prior to fully implementing the troubled asset purchase program. The first definition of troubled assets (Part A) eligible for the TARP program is any

> ... residential or commercial mortgages and any securities, obligations, or other instruments that are based on or related to such mortgages, that in each case was originated or issued on or before March 14, 2008, the purchase of which the Secretary determines promotes financial market stability.

To purchase these assets, Treasury must publish the mechanisms for purchasing assets, pricing and valuation models, the process of choosing asset managers, and the method of identifying troubled assets for purchase.

Some steps have been completed for the purchase of complex mortgage-related securities. Treasury selected Bank of New York-Mellon as the master custodian for the program. Treasury and the Bank of New York have sought to design the auction process and identify which assets to purchase. Treasury chose PricewaterhouseCoopers LLP and Ernst & Young to provide accounting assistance for the program. Treasury has also begun the process of hiring asset managers.

Treasury claims to be working with bank regulators to coordinate the wholeloan purchase program (which is distinct from complex mortgage-backed securities). Mr. Kashkari testified that TARP has reviewed over 100 whole loan asset manager proposals and expects to hire asset managers soon. Given the large share of funds pledged to the capital purchase program, it remains to be seen how much of the TARP program will be dedicated to whole loans.

Once Treasury implements the troubled asset purchase program, institutions will have to conform to program requirements in order to participate. Participating institutions must sell, or commit to sell, to Treasury warrants for nonvoting common or preferred stock (or voting stock if Treasury agrees not to vote). In addition to providing warrants, participating institutions must agree to limits on executive compensation.

On November 12, the Secretary of the Treasury indicated that, in Treasury's assessment, purchasing troubled assets was "not the most effective way to use TARP funds."[19] The Secretary did indicate that the Treasury would be continuing to examine whether asset purchases might be useful in the future. It is unclear to what degree the infrastructure discussed above to provide for asset purchases will be retained or whether it would need to be reconstituted if a future decision were made to purchase troubled assets.

Asset Insurance

Treasury began the notice and comment rulemaking procedure for the insurance program on October 14, 2008. Rather than providing a specific insurance plan, Treasury's notice asked questions to guide the creation of the troubled asset insurance program. Should the insurance program include both whole loans and complex securities? Should the program differ by which particular asset is troubled, and if so, how is that to be measured? How could Home Equity Lines of Credit (HELOC) and other junior liens be addressed in an insurance program? Comments on these and similar questions were due to Treasury by October 28, 2008. Given the focus on capital purchase, discussed below, it is unclear how quickly the Treasury will act to create the insurance program. Section 102 of P.L. 110-343 clearly requires that an insurance program be created, but sets no timelines on its operation.

Preferred Share Purchase

Although some may not have anticipated the purchase of preferred shares to recapitalize the banks, some policymakers had urged this approach from the beginning. Authority to purchase the preferred shares of banks comes under Part B of the definition of troubled asset, which gives Treasury broad discretion in consultation with the Federal Reserve. This announcement came after European authorities announced that they were taking steps to inject capital into their banks.

On October 14, 2008, Treasury announced a voluntary Capital Purchase Program to purchase up to $250 billion of senior preferred shares in financial institutions. The initial nine banks were to receive $125 billion with the additional $125 billion available to other banks wishing to participate. Banks seeking capital use a single application form but submit it to their primary regulator (Federal Reserve, the FDIC, the OCC or the OTS). Once a regulator has reviewed an application, it will send the application and its recommendation to the Office of Financial Stability at the Treasury Department. Treasury says that it will give considerable weight to the regulators' recommendations and decide whether or not to make the capital purchase.

On October 29, the Treasury released data[20] on the Capital Purchase Program indicating it had purchased $125 billion in preferred shares from the banks listed in **Table 1**.

On November 17, the Treasury released further data detailing transactions with a number of smaller banks who had sought assistance. Twenty-one banks were included in the second group with a total of $33.6 billion of shares being purchased. The amount purchased ranged from $9 million to $6.6 billion, with the largest amount going to U.S. Bankcorp.[21] The initial applications for Treasury capital purchase were limited to publicly held corporations, which limited the ability of many smaller institutions, such as private partnerships or mutual institutions, to apply. The Treasury addressed also this concern on November 17, releasing a term sheet of additional information for privately held institutions interested in applying.

In addition to purchasing shares in banks, the Treasury announced on November 10 that the Capital Purchase Program was being used to restructure the financial support provided to AIG, which had previously been provided exclusively by the Federal Reserve. Although AIG's primary business is insurance, which is state regulated, the company itself is a thrift holding company underneath the federal Office of Thrift Supervision, thus making AIG eligible for the program which is generally limited to federally regulated financial institutions. As part of the AIG restructuring, the Treasury will purchase $40 billion in preferred shares, which will pay a 10% dividend.

Homeowners' Assistance

One criticism leveled at TARP has been its focus on assisting financial institutions, providing only indirect assistance to individual homeowners facing foreclosure. The Chairman of the FDIC, in testimony before Congress, indicated that the FDIC saw "significant promise"[22] in using authority in TARP to prevent foreclosures by providing loan guarantees as an incentive to servicers to modify loans. The FDIC and the Treasury indicated they were working on this approach to provide assistance to homeowners. Recent press reports have provided details on a possible approach,[23] but detailed information has not been released by the Treasury on the subject. President Bush's press secretary indicated on October 30, 2008, that an announcement on a mortgage assistance plan was "not imminent."[24] The Secretary of the Treasury indicated in questioning before the House Financial Services Committee on November 18 that he did not expect to use TARP funding to directly prevent foreclosures.

Automobile Manufacturers

Non-financial industries have also sought government support. Most notably, the U.S. automobile industry has argued that disruptions in financial markets have made it even more difficult for consumers to purchase cars. Treasury did not provide TARP funds to manufacturers, arguing that the program is to buy assets from financial institutions. Congress considered, but did not pass, an amendment to EESA that would have directed Treasury to use TARP funds to aid the automobile industry (S. 3688).

Table 1. Initial Treasury Share Purchases Under the Capital Purchase Program

Name of Institution	Amount of Share Purchase
Bank of America	$15 billion
Bank of New York Mellon	$3 billion
Citigroup	$25 billion
Goldman Sachs	$10 billion
JPMorgan Chase	$25 billion
Morgan Stanley	$10 billion
State Street	$2 billion
Wells Fargo	$25 billion
Merrill Lynch	$10 billion

Source: U.S. Treasury.

Consumer Asset-Backed Securities

On November 25, the Treasury announced that TARP funds would be used to purchase securities backed by nonmortgage debts.[25] This asset-backed security (ABS) facility is designed to provide support for consumer purchases and small business spending. Treasury argued that the securitization of credit card receivables, auto loans, student loans, and similar consumer spending shut down in October. Treasury is coordinating its ABS program with the Federal Reserve's Term Asset Backed Securities Loan Facility. Treasury will provide $20 billion of credit protection to the $200 billion facility and announced that it could expand the program to include residential and commercial mortgage securities.

POTENTIAL CAUSES OF FINANCIAL INSTABILITY

EESA authorized a flexible program to respond to financial instability. Treasury has announced that it will implement TARP using a combination of the activities authorized by the act. As the previous discussion has shown, TARP programs can help banks by removing bad assets or injecting capital. TARP programs can also be used to insure bad assets or to directly assist mortgage borrowers. The following section analyzes the TARP program by first discussing potential sources of financial turmoil in general and then discussing some characteristics of the current turmoil that might be addressed by various TARP initiatives.

Financial markets serve as intermediaries between savers and borrowers. If they are running effectively, funds from investors are allocated to borrowers according to their willingness and ability to repay the loans, adjusted for risk. Over the course of a lifetime, most people will have extended periods of being a borrower and of being a saver. Financial markets help young people pay for college and buy their first home, and financial markets help when it comes time to retire. However, if financial markets are disrupted then both savers and borrowers will be frustrated. At times, market imperfections might cause financial markets to under-price risk, which might cause assets to become overpriced (bubbles).[26] At other times, market imperfections might also cause financial markets to over-price risk, which tends to restrict economic activity and possibly trigger recessions. The difficulty for policymakers is to identify market practices that might tend to over-price or under-price risk.

Financial markets are subject to a number of imperfections, some of which are described below. In each case, private firms can attempt to address the problem through contract mechanisms, and policymakers can attempt to address the problem through regulation or other tools. Because private contract is such a flexible device, financial markets are constantly evolving. The evolution of financial instruments and markets can make it difficult for policymakers to identify, monitor, and neutralize potential weaknesses. Some important imperfections are detailed below.

Confidence and the Credit Cycle

Financial intermediaries often practice fractional reserve lending. That is, they keep some fraction of their total assets available for contingencies and use the rest for lending. Because of this fractional reserve system, financial intermediaries are often in a position in which they could not immediately respond to all partners if everyone demanded their funds or other assets at the same time. Even if the firm's assets are much greater than liabilities (the firm is solvent) the firm might not be able to exchange those assets to satisfy immediate costs (the firm is illiquid). Unfortunately, prudence and risk move in opposite directions. The smaller the amount of reserves the intermediary keeps on hand, the greater the potential for profit, but the greater the risk that the firm will be caught without adequate funds if conditions change. Leverage, thus, works in both directions.

To compensate for exposure to intermediaries with inadequate reserves, people may ask business partners to post a bond. The required bond generally declines the more confident people are. As a result, periods of investor confidence and investor pessimism can become self-fulfilling. Confidence tends to expand available credit, which tends to bid up prices, which tends to make the projects more likely to succeed, for a while. Lack of confidence tends to dry up credit, which makes it harder for people to conduct economic activities, which makes it harder for projects to succeed.

The vulnerability of the credit cycle to bouts of overconfidence or panic may be an inherent market failure. One role of a regulator is to monitor reserve assets of financial intermediaries to make sure the latter do not become overextended during times of confidence. In hindsight, it appears that many financial firms became overextended during 2002-2005. Some have called for trying to adjust reserve requirements, leverage, and similar characteristics to "lean against the wind." In this view, regulations should increase capital requirements during boom times and lower them in periods of contraction.

In the current situation, which is discussed in more detail below, banks have experienced both liquidity problems and capital adequacy (solvency) problems. The complexity of MBS has contributed to the difficulty in exchanging these assets, which makes MBS less liquid for anyone who holds them or who might buy them. In addition, default rates on mortgage loans have increased significantly; higher than expected loan losses reduce bank capital. These effects are not mutually exclusive; undercapitalized banks find it more difficult to borrow funds, which means they are less liquid. The asset purchase and asset insurance portions of TARP more directly address liquidity issues,[27] whereas the preferred stock purchase plan more directly addresses solvency issues.

Information Asymmetries

It is often the case in financial contracts that one party has more information than another. It may be the case that there is a group of assets, only some of which are defective. If the seller can identify the defective assets but the buyer cannot, then there is said to be a "market for lemons" and the value of all of the assets will be discounted by potential buyers. Private firms can try to solve the problem through guarantees and similar contract terms. In addition, there may be a role for government inspectors or mandatory disclosures. Regulation of ratings agencies could arguably fall under this category. If a large pool of assets emerges where the assets are unrated because some unknown portion of them are thought to be defective, it may minimize total costs to have an institution with a long time horizon, such as government, acquire the assets and sort quality assets from troubled assets at a later date.

For financial institutions, asymmetric information problems can also be a factor when designing rescue plans. For example, if the originator of loans tends to keep some but sell others on the secondary market then there may be an information problem. The originators may tend to keep the good loans in their own portfolios and pass along the bad loans to others. Similarly, if policymakers offer to acquire assets, firms may try to keep the good assets and sell the bad assets.

In the current situation, the complexity of MBS may have created a lemons problem. Some policymakers are concerned that a program to buy assets from banks will allow banks to "overcharge" the government for their assets. In this view, once the government establishes a price for the assets, only firms who know that their assets are worth less than the price will participate. To prevent the lemons problems, some have suggested an auction process to ensure that assets are priced correctly.[28] If auctions correctly price assets, this program might help remove illiquid assets from bank balance sheets. However, it could be argued that correctly pricing troubled assets is not the only policy goal. Treasury may wish to use the lemons problem with the express purpose of removing the most troubled assets from the bank balance sheets; furthermore, paying more than the current assessed price might also address the policy goal of recapitalizing banks.

Another information problem is what is known as the "winner's curse." In a winner's curse some of the potential bidders have more information than others. Unsophisticated bidders try to free ride on the information provided by the more sophisticated. People watch the "smart" people bid and copy them.

The problem in this is that the "smart" people will know when to stop bidding. Unfortunately, the "winners" will continue bidding for a while, unaware that the sophisticated have stopped participating. As a result, assets become overpriced and could become subject to crashes. Some believe that the process of creating MBS (securitization) was subject to a winner's curse. It might be a role for regulators to limit the right to bid in some circumstances to sophisticated parties or require participants to conduct a minimum of due diligence.

Moral Hazard

Moral hazard occurs when someone has the incentive to take fewer risks prior to an agreement, but the agreement itself creates an incentive for them to take more risks, against the interests of their contracting party. For example, insurance often causes moral hazard so insurance companies often insist that people pay deductibles, install smoke alarms, do not live in a flood plain, and the like. If policymakers rescue some firms then the perception of a safety net may encourage other firms to take on more risk. Similarly, if firms approach insolvency with only a low probability of survival, they might take extremely large risks.

In the current situation, some are concerned that the TARP program could cause moral hazard. Once financial institutions know that the government will spend large sums to remove bad assets or inject additional capital, they may be willing to take additional risks. EESA attempts to deal with moral hazard in part by limiting the compensation that the executives of participating financial institutions can receive. One of the limits specifically prohibits executive compensation that is linked to excessive risk taking during the period that Treasury holds a debt or equity interest in the financial institution (Section 11(B)(2)(a)).

Network Externalities

In some instances, firms can compete in one arena but be network partners in another. For example, sports teams compete on the field and for players and coaches but a sports team must have other sports teams in order to have a marketable entertainment product. Similarly, financial institutions compete in many areas but also must cooperate to clear checks, exchange securities, and manage risk. A trading exchange cannot operate without multiple parties. Furthermore, the greater the number of people that participate, the more liquid the market will be, which in turn increases the value of participating in the exchange. These network externalities can cause coordination problems when the interests of participants conflict. One role for policymakers may be to help resolve network externalities. In the present circumstances, the coordination of trading complex derivatives is arguably one concern of policymakers when considering financial market intervention. TARP may help address this problem by allowing Treasury to consider removing complex derivatives that may pose systemic risks.

Collective Action

Resolving the aforementioned vulnerabilities in financial markets may be in the interests of all financial firms. But it may not be in the interest of any single firm or group of firms to pay all the costs of resolving problems. In these instances, it may be the role of policymakers to help coordinate solutions to collective action problems. The role may be as simple as making information available or gathering parties to facilitate negotiations, or the role may be to provide investment in the infrastructure of the markets themselves. In the present circumstances, both the Federal Reserve and Treasury have been active in attempting to find acquisition partners for troubled financial institutions believed to pose systemic risks. This coordination role may have been helpful in finding a way to unwind the assets of Bear Stearns, but was not successful in similar action for Lehman Brothers.[29]

Sources of Current Market Turmoil

Although the prior section addressed financial market problems in general terms, this section discusses problems specific to the current episode of financial turmoil. The initial spark for the financial turmoil is generally agreed to be the increase in defaults among subprime mortgage borrowers and the loss of liquidity of securities backed by mortgage loans. Since August 2007, financial firms have suffered repeated problems in disposing of "toxic" assets, rolling over their own debt, identifying the relative financial health of potential trading partners, and recapitalizing their balance sheets.[30] The primary tools of the Federal Reserve address liquidity, but financial firms are also experiencing capital adequacy problems. For Fannie Mae and Freddie Mac, the Federal Housing Finance Agency (FHFA, formerly OFHEO) and Treasury helped with both liquidity and capital adequacy for institutions the government deems essential.[31] Some argue that the apparent flip-flop between aid for Bear

Stearns, no aid for Lehman Brothers, and then the subsequent rescue of AIG increased rather than decreased uncertainty. At any rate, credit markets suffered a near collapse in the days after the Lehman Brothers and AIG episodes.

Expectations, Mortgage Defaults, and Asset Prices

If investors expect high default rates by borrowers then prices might adjust to compensate for increased losses; therefore, high default rates by themselves do not necessarily lead to financial market turmoil as long as prices reflect the elevated risk. The rapid rate of increase in defaults on subprime mortgages, however, was unexpected by many investors in global mortgage-backed securities markets.[32] During the early stages of the mortgage market turmoil, some believed that it was largely a subprime problem caused by predatory practices of unregulated lenders.[33] Others argued that there were more general problems in mortgage markets, both prime and subprime, that had encouraged the use of nontraditional mortgage products to speculate on house price appreciation.[34] If the only problem was wrong estimates of default rates then financial markets might be expected to restore stability once higher risk levels are incorporated in prices. Unfortunately, this has not as yet occurred, perhaps in part because there are characteristics of housing markets that tend to reinforce downward price pressures, which also tend to increase default rates.[35]

Evidence of default rates by type of mortgage is consistent with the view that unexpectedly high default rates were not confined to the subprime market. First, defaults are concentrated in formerly rapidly appreciating regions. Second, the default rate on prime adjustable-rate mortgages (ARMs) has increased more rapidly than the default rate on subprime ARMs. At the same time, subprime fixed-rate mortgages are performing better than they had before the housing boom, suggesting that there are issues related to ARMs. **Figure 1** constructs an index (base equals 2001) of the default rates on ARMs, for fixed-rate mortgages, subprime mortgages, and FHA mortgages. Market participants who might have expected default rates to continue would have missed by a greater margin on prime ARMs than on subprime ARMs. Note that the absolute level of default rates is much higher on subprime loans than on prime loans; however, because higher interest rates for riskier loans compensate partially for default risk, the relative change in a given default rate compared to its history is arguably more important to an investor than the absolute default rate. If so, then **Figure 1** and **Figure 2** show that investors in MBS did not just experience a subprime problem, they experienced an ARM problem.

Prices for MBS have been affected by changing views of housing markets. Early in the turmoil, many observers believed that problem loans were largely a subprime phenomenon. However, falling house prices in California, Florida, and several other formerly booming states have exacerbated default rates among all categories of borrowers in those regions. One contributing factor is that mortgage debts exceed the market value of some borrowers homes; therefore, some of these borrowers are increasingly tempted to walk away from their mortgages. As a result, some investors consider a wider class of MBS tainted and these assets are harder to sell at any price. When mortgage problems were considered only a subprime problem, few thought that Fannie Mae or Freddie Mac had a great deal of exposure to problem loans.[36] Subsequently, problems in the broader market have shown that Fannie Mae and Freddie Mac had more problem loans than originally thought. Because housing markets and financial markets are linked, many have expressed skepticism that financial markets will recover before housing markets stabilize.

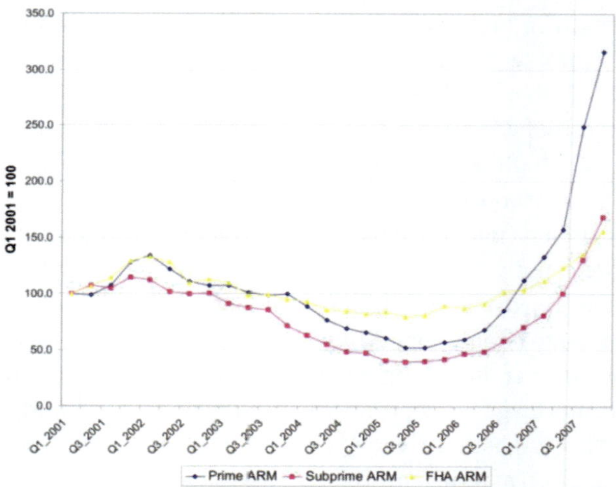

Source: Mortgage Bankers Association National Delinquency Survey.

Figure 1. Index of ARM Foreclosure Rates, 2001=100 Prime ARMs Have Unexpectedly High Foreclosure Rates

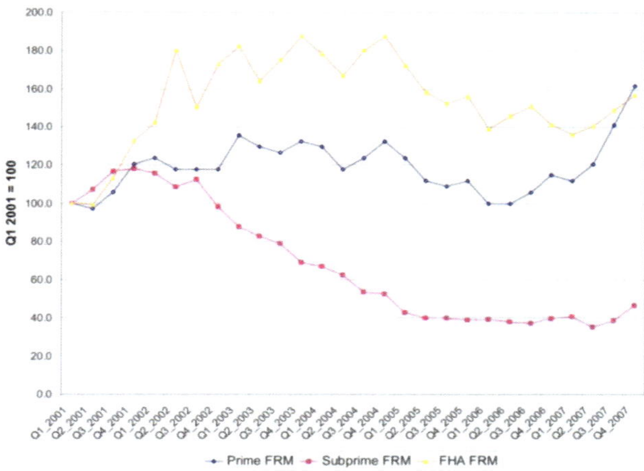

Source: Mortgage Bankers Association National Delinquency Survey.

Figure 2. Index of FRM Foreclosure Rates, 2001=100 Fixed-Rate Subprime Loans Have Unexpectedly Low Foreclosure Rates

Liquidity and Uncertainty

Loss of liquidity has been one of several problems in financial markets since the beginning of what originally became known as the subprime crisis. Liquidity refers to the ability to sell an asset quickly without suffering a significant price reduction — cash is typically the most liquid asset. A firm is liquid if it has a significant portion of its assets in liquid form or can easily access debt markets to acquire liquid assets as needed. A firm is solvent if the value of its assets is greater than the value of its liabilities. An insolvent firm can be in trouble even if all of its assets are perfectly liquid, such as in cash. When mortgage-related securities held by investment banks and other financial firms suffered higher than expected default rates, the MBS lost their liquidity in part because potential buyers were uncertain as to which securities contained the loans that were unlikely to perform. Complex accounting rules which allowed certain assets to be held off-balance sheet made the uncertainty worse, and many mortgage-related securities became illiquid.

Policymakers attempted to restore liquidity to MBS markets over the past year. The Federal Reserve increased liquidity to markets in general by lowering interest rates. It provided liquidity to targeted financial firms by expanding the list of institutions that could directly access the discount window and by providing regular liquidity auctions.[37] The Federal Reserve also attempted to increase the liquidity of mortgage-related assets by adding them to the list of collateral that it would accept for loans. The government tried to increase the liquidity of mortgages by increasing the conforming loan limit (the maximum size loan that the GSEs may purchase). Despite these efforts, financial markets continue to experience significant turmoil.

Capital Adequacy and Leverage

Efforts to restore liquidity do not necessarily address capital adequacy or solvency problems. A relatively small drop in the market value of a firm's assets can cause significant capital reduction if the firm is highly leveraged. Leverage refers to the ratio of a firm's equity capital to its other assets. The greater this ratio the more vulnerable the firm is to falling asset prices. If a firm is leveraged 10:1 and it has $100 in assets then it has $10 in equity capital and $90 in liabilities. In this case, a 5% drop in the value of the firm's assets would reduce assets to $95 (results from a $5 loss). Because assets equal liabilities plus owners equity, and liabilities have not changed, the $5 loss comes out of equity capital. The firms equity would drop from $10 to $5, still solvent in this example. If the firm had been leveraged 25:1 instead of 10:1, then the firm would start with $100 in assets, $96 in liabilities, and $4 in owner's equity. The same 5% drop in asset values would completely wipe out owner's equity and cause the firm to be insolvent (-$1 equity). A key principle of financial markets is that highly leveraged firms can become insolvent for relatively small decreases in asset values; therefore, the damage to the financial system from nonperforming loans can be several times the increase in default rates.[38]

Policymakers have encouraged the financial sector to attempt to rebuild equity capital. Early in the financial crisis, hedge funds and sovereign wealth funds invested in some troubled U.S. financial firms. Investment banks may prove more difficult to recapitalize than commercial banks. Regulation does not specify minimum capital standards for investment banks. Their leverage ratio is largely limited by the confidence, or lack thereof, that financial markets have in them. When market confidence drops for financials, these firms risk their liquidity drying up. If, at the same time that they lose liquidity, they happen to be undercapitalized or near insolvent, then they may not survive.

A number of factors contributed to the increase in leverage in recent years, and the process of reducing leverage may be difficult. One factor that contributed to the increase in leverage during 2002-2005 was low interest rates across the globe, which made it very easy to use short-term debt to finance risky activities.[39] Another factor was the increased use of structured finance (securitization), which allowed banks and other loan originators to move assets off of their balance sheets even though they were still exposed to some risk if the loans failed to perform as expected.[40] A third factor contributing to leverage was the use of complex financial derivatives, which had the potential to reduce financial risks but also had the potential to increase financial risk.

Too Complex to Fail?

Complex financial derivatives have been characterized by some observers as financial weapons of mass destruction. A financial derivative is a contract in which two (or more) parties agree to a payment if a referenced financial instrument changes price or otherwise satisfies conditions set in the contract.[41] Examples of financial derivatives include interest rate swaps and foreign exchange swaps that help firms that are exposed to interest rate risk or exchange rate risk hedge against unexpected market events. The contracts are typically tradable, which has benefits for the market as a whole as well as for the two firms entering into the contract. The ability to trade the derivatives grants the two parties a more liquid asset. The ability to trade the derivatives also provides information to the market as a whole because the observed price of the contracts is a clue to market expectations about the future movements of interest rates, exchange rates, etc. A cost to this increased liquidity is that linkages among firms through the derivative contracts can become very complex and it may become difficult for parties to assess whether their counterparties can actually honor all of their derivative contracts.[42]

The complexity of derivatives contracts has made policymakers uncertain as to the repercussions of allowing a major participant in financial derivatives markets to fail. One worry is that there would be a long period of uncertainty during the unwinding of the derivatives contracts that could potentially freeze global financial markets. In two previous episodes, policymakers chose to facilitate the unwinding of the derivatives contracts. During the Russian debt crisis, the Federal Reserve facilitated the unwinding of Long Term Capital Management (LTCM), although the Federal Reserve did not directly provide funding.[43] For Bear Stearns, the Federal Reserve helped arrange an acquisition by J.P. Morgan, and the Federal Reserve also helped provide the financing.[44] One interpretation of the current market is that policymakers treated AIG as too complex to fail because of the potential difficulty in unwinding their derivatives.[45] AIG is a major participant in credit default swaps, which are derivatives tied to credit losses.

Evidence of the Real Effects of Financial Market Turmoil

Troubles in financial markets do not always spill over into other economic sectors, such as industrial production, agriculture, services, or other parts of the broader economy. Because the current turmoil has lasted more than a year while national unemployment had remained relatively low by historical standards (although rising) and economic growth remained positive (although low) for much of that time, some have questioned whether there is evidence that the current financial turmoil has had significant real effects. Third quarter 2008 growth has been preliminarily assessed by the Commerce Department as negative. Although the fall in house prices could directly reduce consumer spending by making home owners feel poorer (a socalled wealth effect), most economists consider the primary way that financial market turmoil affects the broader economy to be by making it more difficult to get loans, which restricts business investment and consumer purchases of durable goods. The evidence of such effects is thought to be largely in financial market spreads, the difference between the interest rate on less risky debt such as U.S. Treasuries, and the rates paid by banks, firms, and consumers. Interest rate spreads remained elevated after August 2007, even in the inter-bank market where banks lend to each other. Treasury's initial draft for the TARP program was developed the weekend following the large spike in interest rate spreads on September 14, 2008.

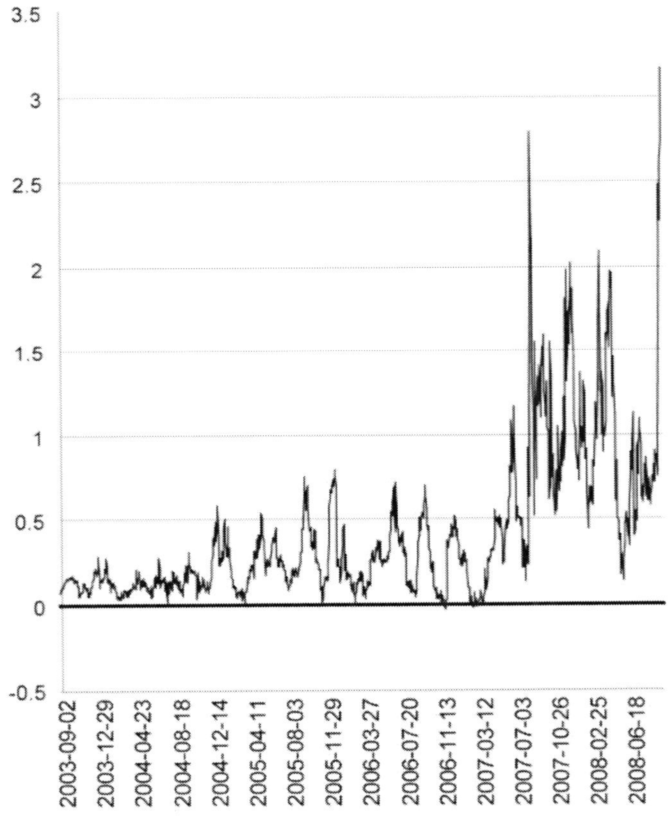

Source: The Federal Reserve.

Figure 3. Spread Between Commercial Paper and One-Month Treasuries

Interest rates can be an indicator of financial market spillovers. The rates at which market participants borrow is typically above the rate that the U.S. government borrows (although not all governments enjoy low borrowing costs). The difference between market rates and the U.S. government rate for a debt of similar maturity, called a spread, can be an indicator of the degree of confidence that market participants have in each other (among other factors). A wide spread can be an indicator of a lack of confidence whereas narrow spreads can be an indicator that markets do not demand a high risk premium. **Figure 3** shows the spread between commercial paper, one form of short-term private loan used mostly by large, highquality corporations, and short-term

Treasury securities. In **Figure 3**, the spread remains relatively narrow from September 2003 until August 2007, which is considered the beginning of the liquidity crunch. The spread on commercial paper spiked in August 2007, remained volatile during the next year, and then spiked again in September 2008. The financial market interventions between August 2007 and September 2008 apparently failed to restore market confidence; as a result, private borrowers continued to pay high interest rates even as interest rates on U.S. Treasury debt declined. The spike in September of 2008 occurred during the week of the interventions for Lehman Brothers and AIG.

Wealth Effect?

A wealth effect refers to the tendency of people to spend in the current period at least part of any increase in wealth that they receive. When asset prices rise, such as houses, stocks and bonds in retirement accounts, collectible art, or similar savings instruments, people may feel wealthier. When house prices were booming, consumer spending was supplemented by mortgage equity withdrawal to access households' perceived increase in wealth. Now that house prices have stopped rising nationally, and are falling significantly in some areas, mortgage equity withdrawal has no longer been contributing much to consumer spending. In some cases, lenders have been seeking to cancel or reduce lines of credit they had extended on homes. Although falling house prices could possibly have a negative wealth effect, few people fully tapped their home equity so the reduction in the lines of credit is not widely expected to have a large effect. Furthermore, according to the Mortgage Bankers Association National Delinquency Survey, 97% of home owners are not in the foreclosure process, and aggregate consumer spending levels did not decline for the first year of financial turmoil (although consumer spending growth was below trend). Whether due to rising unemployment, a wealth effect from falling house prices, the stock market declines in the Fall of 2008, or other factors, third quarter consumer spending is estimated to have declined.

Bank Balance Sheets and Tightening Credit Markets

Rather than working directly through consumer spending, financial market turmoil is generally considered to affect the broader economy by reducing the availability of credit to firms and consumers. Rising default rates and falling asset prices reduce the value of the assets on bank balance sheets. As discussed above, banks are leveraged so that a fall in the value of their assets can significantly damage their capital. Falling house prices have the potential to cause mortgage lenders both liquidity and solvency problems. In response, banks may become hesitant to part with cash and may therefore choose to tighten their lending standards. Low risk borrowers may be able to qualify for loans, possibly even at low interest rates, but many higher risk loans might not be granted at any interest rate. It is possible to observe low interest rates in these circumstances with relatively little actual lending taking place.

The evidence in the current market is consistent with tightening lending standards and reduced credit availability. The survey of bank lending managers showed tightening lending standards since the beginning of the financial market turmoil. Reductions in the Federal Reserve's policy interest rate have not, as yet, been followed by loosening lending standards. Spreads between Treasury rates and consumer loans, such as mortgage rates, remained elevated so that the reduction in the Fed's rate provided little relief to borrowers facing an increase in their mortgage rate.

The TARP program can strengthen bank balance sheets in several ways. Under TARP, Treasury can directly inject capital into the bank balance sheet though the preferred share stock purchase program. This creates a larger cushion between a bank's current standing and insolvency. TARP also enables the Treasury to remove troubled assets from bank balance sheets, This increases the institution's liquidity, but does less for bank solvency. TARP can also allow financial institutions to insure their troubled assets, which would make those assets more liquid, but may also do little for bank solvency. TARP permits direct assistance to homeowners, which would presumably be aimed at reducing default rates. Reducing default rates by fully paying loans could in theory simultaneously remove the stigma of mortgage-related assets, increase their price and their liquidity, and restore some bank capital.

Reinforcing Delinquencies and Foreclosures in Housing Markets

Tight lending standards tend to reinforce delinquencies and foreclosures. Some borrowers may have taken out large mortgages when credit was easy and rates were low, with the intent of refinancing their loans before maturity. Tightening lending standards reduce their ability to refinance on favorable terms and make it less likely that they can keep their house. Not only do tight lending markets reduce the ability of current residents to pay their loans, but strict lending standards also make it less likely that a third party can be found to purchase the house. As a result, foreclosures can add to the unsold inventory of homes, which tends to drive down prices and further depress bank balance sheets. Some fear that this process can become selfreinforcing because rising delinquencies might also result in tight lending conditions.

Difficulties of Using Debt Financing to Fund Purchases

There are also other assets besides housing for which demand depends on the ability of buyers to find financing. Some municipalities had depended on the ability to roll over short term debt in the form of auction-rate securities. When financial markets froze, some auctions failed to attract enough bidders to continue rolling over the debt. As a result, the interest rates paid increased significantly. Complaints by some municipalities that the risks of these investment instruments were not fully disclosed has led several investment banks to agree to take back the securities on to their own balance sheets (which may already be under significant stress).[46] The automobile market has also suffered as automakers canceled some leasing programs. Student loans have also become harder to get, although some believe that this is be due at least in part, to a change in the federal funding formula.[47]

CONCLUSION

The EESA authorizes Treasury to spend up to $700 billion to restore financial stability. In general, there are at least five policy responses to a banking disruption: (1) removing bad assets from bank balance sheets, (2) injecting capital into the banking system, (3) insuring "toxic" assets, (4) directing support of delinquent borrowers to reduce default rates, and (5) allowing the free market time to liquidate troubled assets and process insolvent institutions. The breadth of the definition of a troubled asset under the TARP statute grants Treasury the discretion to implement any of these options individually or in combination. Although Treasury's original proposal focused on option 1 (removing bad assets), the majority of TARP funding to date has been more consistent with option 2 (injecting capital). Using the majority of

TARP funds for capital injection matches the approach taken by several European nations in response to their banking turmoil.

APPENDIX. GLOSSARY OF TERMS RELATED TO DISRUPTION OF FINANCIAL MARKETS

Adverse Selection — When a party having greater information about the quality of a pool of assets offers to sell the inferior ones to the less knowledgeable party.

AIG — American International Group, Inc.

ARM — Adjustable Rate Mortgage.

Bank holding companies — Companies that own one or more banks.

Bubble — Self-reinforcing process in which the price of an asset exceeds its fundamental value for a sustained period. Often followed by a rapid price decline.

Conservatorship — When an insolvent financial institution is reorganized by a regulator with the intent to restoring it to an ongoing business.

CDO, Collateralized Debt Obligation — Securities deriving their income from other fixed income assets, including but not limited to, mortgage-related assets.

CDS, Credit Default Swap — A tradeable contract in which one party agrees to pay another if a third party experiences a credit event, such as bankruptcy or credit downgrade.

Credit Event — In a credit default swap, an event specified in the contract that triggers the payment between the parties. Is often a bankruptcy or credit downgrade.

Credit Risk — The risk that a borrower will fail to repay a loan in full.

EESA — Emergency Economic Stabilization Act, P.L. 110-343.

FASB — Financial Accounting Standards Board.

FAS 157 — An accounting standard issued by FASB that covers the reporting of the fair value of financial assets. Determines if financial assets must be marked-tomarket.

FDIC — Federal Deposit Insurance Corporation.

FHA — Federal Housing Administration.

FHFA — Federal Housing Finance Agency.

Financial Derivatives — Investment products that derive their payments from previously issued securities.

FRM — Fixed Rate Mortgage.

Hedge Funds — Unregulated mutual funds that buy and sell investment assets.

HELOC — Home Equity Line of Credit.

Insolvent — When a firm's liabilities are greater than assets.

LTCM — Long Term Capital Management.

Leverage Ratio — Ratio of a firm's capital to its assets.

Liquidity — The ability to trade an asset quickly without significantly reducing its price, or the ability of a person or firm to access credit markets.

Mark-to-Market — The accounting requirement to report assets held for sale at current market prices. Related to FAS 157.

MBS, Mortgage Backed Security — A security which derives its payments from a pool of mortgage obligations.

Moral Hazard — The tendency of people to take more risks once another party has agreed to provide protection.

Notional Principal — In a swap contract, the amount on which the interest is being paid (for interest rate swaps) or the protection payment is calculated (for credit default swaps).

OCC — Office of the Comptroller of the Currency.

OFHEO — Office of Federal Housing Enterprise Oversight.

OTC, Over-the-Counter Market — Unregulated market in which dealers at different locations stand ready to trade securities with anyone willing to accept the prices.

OTS — Office of Thrift Supervision.

Preferred Stock — Receives a fixed dividend and must be paid before common stock but typically does not have voting rights.

Prime Borrowers — Borrowers with high credit scores, sufficient down payments, documented income, and other indicators of low credit risk.

Protection Buyer — In a credit default swap, the party that receives payment if a credit event occurs.

Protection Seller — In a credit default swap, the party that makes payment if a credit event occurs.

Receivership — When an insolvent financial institution is taken over with the intent to liquidate its assets.

Risk-Based Capital — An amount of capital a lending institution must keep in reserve based on the riskiness of its assets.

Securitization — The process of transforming a flow of funds, typically from a debt, into a new marketable security.

SEC — Securities and Exchange Commission.

Spreads — The difference between two rates, typically bond yields or interest rates of the same maturity. Wide spreads often indicate lack of market confidence.

Subprime Borrowers — Borrowers with low credit scores and/or other indicators of higher credit risk.

TARP — Troubled Asset Relief Program, created by P.L. 110-343.

End Notes

[1] Division A of H.R. 1424/P.L. 110-343.

[2] CRS Report RS22963, *Financial Market Intervention*, by Edward V. Murphy and Baird Webel.

[3] CRS Report RS22722, *Securitization and Federal Regulation of Mortgages for Safety and Soundness*, by Edward V. Murphy.

[4] See CRS Report RL34420, *Bear Stearns: Crisis and 'Rescue' for a Major Provider of Mortgage-Related Products*, by Gary Shorter, and CRS Report RS22950, *Fannie Mae and Freddie Mac in Conservatorship*, by Mark Jickling.

[5] See CRS Report RS22966, *Financial Turmoil: Comparing the Troubled Assets Relief Program to the Federal Reserve's Response*, by Marc Labonte, for more discussion on the question of liquidity vs. capital adequacy.

[6] One example of this was the Reconstruction Finance Corporation (RFC), a Depression-era program to stabilize the financial sector. In the Hoover administration, RFC primarily lent funds to banks but in the Roosevelt administration the RFC began purchasing preferred stock in banks.

[7] One example of this was the Resolution Trust Corporation, which was used to mitigate the savings and loan failures in the late 1980s; see CRS Report RS22959, *The Resolution Trust Corporation: Historical Analysis*, by Gary Shorter.

[8] Additional provisions included a temporary increase in the limit on FDIC-provided depository insurance, discussed later in this report, as well as the extension of temporary tax provisions, which are not addressed in this report. See CRS Report RL32367, *Certain Temporary Tax Provisions ('Extenders') Expired in 2007*, by Pamela J. Jackson and Jennifer Teefy, and CRS Report RL32554, An Overview of Tax Benefits for Higher Education Expenses, by Pamela J. Jackson and Christian Gonzalez, for more information on some of the tax provisions in P.L. 110-343.

[9] See CRS Report RS22969, *The Emergency Economic Stabilization Act's Insurance for Troubled Assets*, by Baird Webel.

[10] See CRS Report RS20234, *Expedited or 'Fast-Track' Legislative Procedures*, by Christopher M. Davis.

[11] See CRS Report RL34713, *Emergency Economic Stabilization Act: Preliminary Analysis of Oversight Provisions*, and CRS Report RL34740, *Reporting Requirements in the Emergency Economic Stabilization Act of 2008*, both by Curtis W. Copeland.

[12] See CRS Report RL34623, *Housing and Economic Recovery Act of 2008*, by N. Eric Weiss et al.

[13] P.L. 110-142, 121 Stat. 1803.

[14] For more information, see CRS Report RL34212 *Analysis of the Tax Exclusion for Canceled Mortgage Debt Income*, by Mark P. Keightley and Erika Lunder.

[15] For more information see CRS Report RS22987, *National Credit Union Share Insurance Fund (NCUSIF): Credit Union Deposit Insurance, by Pauline Smale and CRS Report RS21987, When Financial Businesses Fail: Protection for Account Holders*, by Walter W. Eubanks.

[16] U.S. Senate, Committee on Finance, "Tax Provisions in Financial Rescue Plan Protect Homeowners and Community Banks," News Release, September 28, 2008, available at:[http://finance.senate.gov/press/Bpress/2008press/prb092808.pdf].

[17] For more information on these tax issues, contact CRS Specialist in Public Finance Thomas Hungerford, Government and Finance Division.

[18] U.S. Department of Treasury,"Remarks by Secretary Henry M. Paulson, Jr. on Financial Rescue Package and Economic Update." press release HP-1265, November 12, 2008.

[19] U.S. Department of Treasury, "Remarks by Secretary Henry M. Paulson, Jr. on Financial Rescue Package and Economic Update," press release, November 12, 2008, available at [http://ustreas.gov/press/releases/hp1265.htm].

[20] U.S. Treasury, Capital Purchase Program Transaction Report, October 29, 2008, available at [http://www.treas.gov/initiatives/eesa/docs/TransactionReport.pdf].

[21] For a complete list, see the "Capital Purchase Program Transaction Report" available on the Treasury website at [http://ustreas.gov/initiatives/eesa/transactions.shtml].

[22] Testimony of Honorable Sheila C. Bair before the U.S. Senate Committee on Banking, "Turmoil in the U.S. Credit Markets: Examining Recent Regulatory Responses," October 23 2008, ava i l able at [ht t p: / / banking. senate.gov/public/_f i les /BAIRCredit Markettestimony102308.pdf].

[23] "Treasury, FDIC Near Deal on Mortgage Aid," *Washington Post*, October 30, 2008, p. A01.

[24] White House Office of the Press Secretary, "Press Briefing by Press Secretary Dana Perino and Council of Economic Advisers Chairman Ed Lazear," October 30, 2008.

[25] "Secretary Paulson Remarks on Consumer ABS Lending Facility," U.S. Department of Treasury Press release HP-1293, November 25, 2008.

[26] CRS Report RL33666, *Asset Bubbles: Economic Effects and Policy Options for the Federal Reserve*, by Marc Labonte.

[27] The impact of the asset insurance and asset purchase programs on solvency depends greatly on the premiums charged for the insurance and the prices paid for the assets.

[28] CRS Report RL34707, *Auction Basics: Background for Assessing Proposed Treasury Purchases of Mortgage-Backed Securities*, by D. Andrew Austin.

[29] CRS Report RL34420, *Bear Stearns: Crisis and 'Rescue' for a Major Provider of Mortgage-Related Products*, by Gary Shorter.

[30] CRS Report RL34182, *Financial Crisis? The Liquidity Crunch of August 2007*, by Darryl E. Getter, Mark Jickling, Marc Labonte, and Edward V. Murphy.

[31] CRS Report RL34661, *Fannie Mae's and Freddie Mac's Financial Problems*, by N. Eric Weiss.

[32] John Kiff and Paul Mills, "Lessons from Subprime Turbulence," IMF *Survey Magazine: IMF Research*, August 23, 2007, available at [http://www.imf.org/external/pubs/ft/survey/so/2007/RES0823A.HTM].

[33] "Testimony of Paul Leanard," California Office Director, Center for Responsible Lending, before the California Senate Banking Committee, March 6, 2007, available at [http://www.responsiblelending.org/pdfs/FINAL-Leonard-3-26-Testimony.pdf].

[34] CRS Report RL33775, *Alternative Mortgages: Causes and Policy Implications of Troubled Mortgage Resets in the Subprime and Alt-A Markets*, by Edward V. Murphy.

[35] CRS Report RL34653, *Economic Analysis of a Mortgage Foreclosure Moratorium*, by Edward V. Murphy.

[36] See for example, Allen Fishbein, Director of Housing and Credit Policy, Consumer Federation of America, "Testimony Before the House Financial Services Committee," March 15, 2007, pp. 6-7, suggesting that the GSEs be encouraged to lead the market among riskier borrower groups, including lower-income, first-time home buyers, and minorities.

[37] CRS Report RL34427, *Financial Turmoil: Federal Reserve Policy Responses*, by Marc Labonte.
[38] CRS Report RL34412, *Averting Financial Crisis*, by Mark Jickling.
[39] CRS Report RL34182, *Financial Crisis? The Liquidity Crunch of August 2007*, by Darryl E. Getter, Mark Jickling, Marc Labonte, and Edward V. Murphy.
[40] CRS Report RS22722, *Securitization and Federal Regulation of Mortgages for Safety and Soundness*, by Edward V. Murphy.
[41] CRS Report RS22918, *Primer on Energy Derivatives and Their Regulation*, by Mark Jickling.
[42] CRS Report RL34420, *Bear Stearns: Crisis and 'Rescue' for a Major Provider of Mortgage-Related Products,* by Gary Shorter.
[43] CRS Report RL33746, *Hedge Fund Failures*, by Mark Jickling.
[44] CRS Report RL34427, *Financial Turmoil: Federal Reserve Policy Responses*, by Marc Labonte.
[45] CRS Report RS22932, *Credit Default Swaps: Frequently Asked Questions*, by Edward V. Murphy.
[46] CRS Report RL34672, *Auction Rate Securities*, by D. Andrew Austin.
[47] CRS Report RL34452, *The Ensuring Continued Access to Student Loans Act of 2008*, by David P. Smole, and CRS Report RL34578, *Economics of Guaranteed Student Loans*, by D. Andrew Austin.

In: Emergency Economic Stabilization Act ISBN: 978-1-60741-327-1
Editor: Nikola Vazquez

Chapter 3

Reporting Requirements in the Emergency Economic Stabilization Act of 2008*

Curtis W. Copeland

Summary

The Emergency Economic Stabilization Act of 2008 (EESA, Division A of H.R. 1424, P.L. 110-343) established numerous reporting requirements regarding a variety of issues. The entities charged with preparation of these reports include both new entities established by the act (e.g., the Financial Stability Oversight Board and the Congressional Oversight Panel) as well as agencies and officials who existed before the enactment of EESA (e.g., the Secretary of the Treasury and the Comptroller General of the United States). The recipients of these reports also vary, as well as their timing, frequency, and factors that trigger their development. These differences notwithstanding, all of the EESA reports appear to share a common purpose — to provide information to Congress and other entities on the implementation of the act's provisions.

---

* This is an edited, reformatted and augmented version of a CRS Report for Congress, Report RL34740 updated November 13, 2008.

No single entity receives all of the EESA-required reports. It is not readily apparent why some of the reports are to be filed with a particular set of eight "appropriate committees," some to a subset of those committees, and some to Congress as a whole. Some of the entities designated to prepare or receive the reports have not been formally established (e.g., the Congressional Oversight Panel and the Special Inspector General). Although one of the purposes of the legislation is to provide "public accountability" for the use of EESA authorities, only one of the reports is required to be made to the public, and it is unclear whether the other reports will ultimately be provided to the public. Some of the reports are required to be submitted very quickly, but other reports are not required for years. Some of the reporting requirements are recurring (e.g., every 30 days, or quarterly), while others are one-time requirements. Most of the requirements include clear starting points for the submission of the reports, but in some cases, the starting points are unclear.

Many of the act's reporting requirements seem to address the same or similar issues. The number and variety of the required reports may have been intended to provide a variety of perspectives on the implementation of EESA, but the lack of integration of those requirements may make understanding the implementation of the act difficult. Also, given the nature of the "troubled assets" currently being purchased under the act (i.e., bank stock instead of mortgages or other instruments related to mortgages), it is unclear whether some of the specific requirements are still relevant. Other information that is not specifically required by the act (e.g., how the federal funds are being used by the recipients) may be more helpful to Congress and others as they conduct oversight of the program. Finally, some of the reporting requirements expire on the date that the last troubled asset is sold or transferred, or the date that the last insurance contract expires. Without some kind of a lag period for these requirements, a complete history of the transactions may not be provided.

This report will be updated when new information becomes available.

The Emergency Economic Stabilization Act of 2008 (EESA, Division A of H.R. 1424, which was enacted on October 3, 2008, as P.L. 110-343) established numerous reporting requirements regarding a variety of issues.[1] Some of the reporting requirements are assigned to newly established entities in the act, including the Financial Stability Oversight Board,[2] the Congressional Oversight Panel (COP),[3] and the Special Inspector General for the Troubled Asset Relief Program (SIG TARP).[4] Other reporting requirements are given to agencies and officials who existed before the enactment of EESA (e.g., the Secretary of the Treasury and the Comptroller

General of the United States).[5] The recipients of these reports also vary, as well as their timing, frequency, and factors that trigger their development. These differences notwithstanding, all of the EESA reports appear to share a common purpose — to provide information to Congress and other entities on the implementation of the act's provisions.

This report describes the various reporting requirements in EESA and is organized according to the entities required to prepare and submit the reports. The report also provides some concluding observations regarding those requirements. The **Appendix** of the report summarizes the act's reporting requirements in terms of those responsible for producing and receiving the reports, the timing of the reports, and when the reports are scheduled to end.

Reports by the Secretary of the Treasury

Section 102(b) (Troubled Asset Relief Program)

Section 101 of EESA authorizes the Secretary of the Treasury "to establish the Troubled Asset Relief Program (or 'TARP') to purchase, and to make and fund commitments to purchase, troubled assets from any financial institution." Section 102(a) states that if the Secretary of the Treasury establishes TARP, "then the Secretary shall establish a program to guarantee troubled assets originated or issued prior to March 14, 2008, including mortgage-backed securities."[6] Section 102(b) says that, "Not later than 90 days after the date of enactment of this Act, the Secretary shall report to the appropriate committees of Congress on the program established under subsection (a)."[7] Section 3(1) of EESA defines the term "appropriate committees of Congress" in the act to mean "(A) the Committee on Banking, Housing, and Urban Affairs, the Committee on Finance, the Committee on the Budget, and the Committee on Appropriations of the Senate; and (B) the Committee on Financial Services, the Committee on Ways and Means, the Committee on the Budget, and the Committee on Appropriations of the House of Representatives."

Section 105(a) (General Reports)

Section 105(a) of the act states that, "Before the expiration of the 60-day period beginning on the date of the first exercise of the authority granted in section 101(a), or of the first exercise of the authority granted in section 102, whichever occurs first, and every 30-day period thereafter, the Secretary [of the Treasury] shall report to the appropriate committees of Congress." Each such report is required to contain

(1) an overview of actions taken by the Secretary, including the considerations required by section 103 and the efforts under section 109;
(2) the actual obligation and expenditure of the funds provided for administrative expenses by section 118 during such period and the expected expenditure of such funds in the subsequent period; and
(3) a detailed financial statement with respect to the exercise of authority under this Act, including (A) all agreements made or renewed; (B) all insurance contracts entered into pursuant to section 102; (C) all transactions occurring during such period, including the types of parties involved; (D) the nature of the assets purchased; (E) all projected costs and liabilities; (F) operating expenses, including compensation for financial agents; (G) the valuation or pricing method used for each transaction; and (H) a description of the vehicles established to exercise such authority.

Section 105(d) of the act requires that this report also be submitted to the COP. Section 105(g) states that this reporting requirement "shall terminate on the later of (1) the date that the last troubled asset acquired by the Secretary under section 101 has been sold or transferred out of the ownership or control of the Federal Government; or (2) the date of expiration of the last insurance contract issued under section 102."

Section 105(b) (Tranche Reports)

Section 105(b)(1) of the act requires the Secretary of the Treasury to provide to the "appropriate committees of Congress"

> a written report, including (A) a description of all of the transactions made during the reporting period; (B) a description of the pricing mechanism for the transactions; (C) a justification of the price paid for and other financial terms associated with the transactions; (D) a description of the impact of the exercise of such authority on the financial system, supported, to the extent possible, by specific data; (E) a description of challenges that remain in the financial system, including any benchmarks yet to be achieved; and (F) an estimate of additional actions under the authority provided under this Act that may be necessary to address such challenges.

Section 105(b)(2) requires this report to be submitted "not later than 7 days after the date on which commitments to purchase troubled assets under the authorities provided in this Act first reach an aggregate of $50,000,000,000 and not later than 7 days after each $50,000,000,000 interval of such commitments is reached thereafter."[8] Section 105(d) of the act requires that this report also be submitted to the COP. Section 105(g) of the act states that this reporting requirement "shall terminate on the later of (1) the date that the last troubled asset acquired by the Secretary under section 101 has been sold or transferred out of the ownership or control of the Federal Government; or (2) the date of expiration of the last insurance contract issued under section 102."

Section 105(c) (Regulatory Modernization Report)

Section 105(c) of the act requires the Secretary of the Treasury to "review the current state of the financial markets and the regulatory system and submit a written report to the appropriate committees of Congress not later than April 30, 2009, analyzing the current state of the regulatory system and its effectiveness at overseeing the participants in the financial markets, including the over-the-counter swaps market and government-sponsored enterprises." Section 105(c) also requires the report to provide "recommendations for improvement, including (1) recommendations regarding (A) whether any participants in the financial markets that are currently outside the regulatory system should become subject to the regulatory system; and (B) enhancement of the clearing and settlement of over-the-counter swaps; and (2) the rationale underlying such recommendations." Section 105(d) of the act requires that this report also be submitted to the COP. Section 105(g) of the act states that this reporting requirement "shall terminate on the later of (1) the date that the last troubled asset acquired by the Secretary under section 101 has been sold or transferred out of the ownership or control of the Federal Government; or (2) the date of expiration of the last insurance contract issued under section 102."

Section 114(a) (Market Transparency, Pricing)

While not a formal reporting requirement, Section 114(a) of the act states that, "To facilitate market transparency, the Secretary shall make available to the public, in electronic form, a description, amounts, and pricing of assets acquired under this Act, within 2 business days of purchase, trade, or other disposition."

Reports by the Financial Stability Oversight Board

Section 104(g)

Section 104(g) of the act requires the Financial Stability Oversight Board to "report to the appropriate committees of Congress and the Congressional Oversight Panel established under section 125, not less frequently than quarterly, on the matters described under subsection (a)(1)." Subsection 104(a)(1) charges the Financial Stability Oversight Board with

> reviewing the exercise of authority under a program developed in accordance with this Act, including (A) policies implemented by the Secretary and the Office of Financial Stability created under sections 101 and 102, including the appointment of financial agents, the designation of asset classes to be purchased, and plans for the structure of vehicles used to purchase troubled assets; and (B) the effect of such actions in assisting American families in preserving home ownership, stabilizing financial markets, and protecting taxpayers.

Although EESA does not establish a sunset date for this reporting requirement, Section 104(h) of the act states that the Financial Stability Oversight Board and its authority "shall terminate on the expiration of the 15-

day period beginning upon the later of (1) the date that the last troubled asset acquired by the Secretary under section 101 has been sold or transferred out of the ownership or control of the Federal Government; or (2) the date of expiration of the last insurance contract issued under section 102."

REPORTS BY THE CONGRESSIONAL OVERSIGHT PANEL

Section 125(b)(1) (Regular Reports)

EESA requires the COP to submit both "regular" reports and a "special" report on regulatory reform to Congress. With regard to the panel's regular reports, Section 125(b)(1)(A) of the act requires that they include

> (i) the use by the Secretary of authority under this Act, including with respect to the use of contracting authority and administration of the program., (ii) the impact of purchases made under the Act on the financial markets and financial institutions; (iii) the extent to which the information made available on transactions under the program has contributed to market transparency; and (iv) the effectiveness of foreclosure mitigation efforts, and the effectiveness of the program from the standpoint of minimizing long-term costs to the taxpayers and maximizing the benefits for taxpayers.

Section 125(b)(1)(B) requires that these reports "be submitted not later than 30 days after the first exercise by the Secretary of the authority under section 101(a) or 102, and every 30 days thereafter."[9] The act does not provide a sunset date for this or other reports by the panel, but Section 125(f) requires the COP to terminate six months after the authorities provided in Sections 101(a)(3) and 102 expire; Section 120 states that those authorities terminate on December 31, 2009. Therefore, the COP and its reporting requirements are scheduled to end on or about June 30, 2010.

Section 125(b)(2) (Special Report on Regulatory Reform)

The act also requires the COP to submit to Congress a "special report on regulatory reform not later than January 20, 2009, analyzing the current state of the regulatory system and its effectiveness at overseeing the participants in the financial system and protecting consumers." The report is also required to provide "recommendations for improvement, including recommendations regarding whether any participants in the financial markets that are currently outside the regulatory system should become subject to the regulatory system, the rationale underlying such recommendation, and whether there are any gaps in existing consumer protections."

REPORTS BY THE SPECIAL INSPECTOR GENERAL

Section 121(f)(1)

Not later than 60 days after the confirmation of the Special Inspector General,[10] and everycalendar quarter thereafter, EESA requires the Special Inspector General to submit to the "appropriate committees of Congress" a report "summarizing the activities of the Special Inspector General during the 120-day period ending on the date of such report." The act goes on to require that each report include, for the period covered by the report, "a detailed statement of all purchases, obligations, expenditures, and revenues associated with any program established by the Secretary of the Treasury under sections 101 and 102, as well as the information collected under subsection (c)(1)." Section 121(f)(3) of the act requires that this report also be submitted to the COP. The act does not provide a sunset date for these reports, but Section 121(h) requires the Office of the Special Inspector General to terminate on the later of (1) the date that the last troubled asset acquired under Section 101 has been sold or transferred, or (2) the date that the last insurance contract under Section 102 expires.

REPORTS BY THE COMPTROLLER GENERAL

Section 116(a)(3) (Oversight Reporting)

Section 116(a)(3) of the act requires the Comptroller General to submit "reports of findings under this section, regularly and no less frequently than once every 60 days, to the appropriate committees of Congress, and the Special Inspector General for the Troubled Asset Relief Program established under this Act on the activities and performance of the TARP."[11] The section also permits the Comptroller to submit "special reports under this subsection as warranted by the findings of its oversight activities." Section 116(d) requires that all of these reports also be sent to the COP. Section 116(2)(C) requires the Department of the Treasury to reimburse GAO for "the full cost of any such oversight activities." Section 116(e) of the act states that the Comptroller General's oversight, auditing, and reporting responsibilities end on "(1) the date that the last troubled asset acquired by the Secretary under section 101 has been sold or transferred out of the ownership or control of the Federal Government; or (2) the date of expiration of the last insurance contract issued under section 102."

Section 116(b) (Audit of TARP Financial Statement)

Section 116(b) of the act requires the TARP to prepare and issue audited financial statements to the appropriate committees of Congress and the public. That section goes on to require the Comptroller General to "annually audit such statements in accordance with generally accepted auditing standards." Therefore, GAO will essentially be auditing the financial statement's audit. The act also requires the Department of the Treasury to "reimburse the Government Accountability Office for the full cost of any such audit."

Section 116(d) requires that these audits be sent to the COP.[12] According to GAO, the GAO audit will also be sent to the "appropriate committees of Congress." Section 116(e) of the act states that this reporting responsibility ends on "(1) the date that the last troubled asset acquired by the Secretary under section 101 has been sold or transferred out of the ownership or control of the Federal Government; or (2) the date of expiration of the last insurance contract issued under section 102."

Section 117 (Margin Authority)

Section 117(a) of the act requires the Comptroller General to "undertake a study to determine the extent to which leverage and sudden deleveraging of financial institutions was a factor behind the current financial crisis." Section 117(b) requires that the content of the study include

(1) an analysis of the roles and responsibilities of the Board, the Securities and Exchange Commission, the Secretary, and other Federal banking agencies with respect to monitoring leverage and acting to curtail excessive leveraging; (2) an analysis of the authority of the Board to regulate leverage, including by setting margin requirements, and what process the Board used to decide whether or not to use its authority; (3) an analysis of any usage of the margin authority by the Board; and (4) recommendations for the Board and appropriate committees of Congress with respect to the existing authority of the Board.

Section 117(c) requires that the Comptroller General complete and submit this report no later than June 1, 2009, to the Committee on Banking, Housing, and Urban Affairs of the Senate and the Committee on Financial Services of the House of Representatives. Section 117(d) requires that this report also be sent to the COP.

Reports by the Office of Management and Budget

Section 134 (Recoupment)

EESA was signed into law on October 3, 2008. Section 134 of the act says that, five years after this date (i.e., October 3, 2013), the Director of the Office of Management and Budget (OMB), in consultation with the Director of the Congressional Budget Office, must "submit a report to the Congress on the net amount within the Troubled Asset Relief Program under this Act." This section goes on to say that, "In any case where there is a shortfall, the President shall submit a legislative proposal that recoups from the financial industry an amount equal to the shortfall in order to ensure that the Troubled Asset Relief Program does not add to the deficit or national debt."

Section 202(a) (Cost of TARP)

Section 202(a) of the act requires OMB (but not specifically the Director) to submit a report to the President and Congress within 60 days of the first exercise of the authority granted in Section 101(a), but in no case later than

December 31, 2008, and semiannually thereafter.[13] These reports are to include

(1) the estimate, notwithstanding section 502(5)(F) of the Federal Credit Reform Act of 1990 (2 U.S.C. 661a(5)(F)), as of the first business day that is at least 30 days prior to the issuance of the report, of the cost of the troubled assets, and guarantees of the troubled assets, determined in accordance with section 123;
(2) the information used to derive the estimate, including assets purchased or guaranteed, prices paid, revenues received, the impact on the deficit and debt, and a description of any outstanding commitments to purchase troubled assets; and
(3) a detailed analysis of how the estimate has changed from the previous report.

As discussed in more detail later in this report, Section 202(b) of the act requires the Congressional Budget Office to provide an assessment of OMB's report. Beginning with the second report, Section 202(a) requires OMB to "explain the differences between the Congressional Budget Office estimates delivered in accordance with subsection (b) and prior Office of Management and Budget estimates."

REPORTS BY THE CONGRESSIONAL BUDGET OFFICE

Section 202(b) (Assessment of OMB Report)

Within 45 days of receipt by Congress of each report from OMB under Section 202(a) of the act, the Congressional Budget Office is required to report to Congress its assessment of OMB's report, including "(1) the cost of the troubled assets and guarantees of the troubled assets, (2) the information and valuation methods used to calculate such cost, and (3) the impact on the deficit and the debt."[14] Section 202(c) of the act states that "In carrying out the duties in this subsection or performing analyses of activities under this Act, the Director of the Congressional Budget Office may employ personnel and procure the services of experts and consultants."

Reports to be Submitted by Others

Section 110(b)(5) (Homeowner Assistance)

Section 110(b) of EESA requires each "Federal property manager" that holds, owns, or controls mortgages, mortgage backed securities, and other assets secured by residential real estate to (among other things) "implement a plan that seeks to maximize assistance for homeowners." Section 110(a)(1) of the act defines a "federal property manager" as

> (A) the Federal Housing Finance Agency, in its capacity as conservator of the Federal National Mortgage Association and the Federal Home Loan Mortgage Corporation; (B) the [Federal Deposit Insurance] Corporation, with respect to residential mortgage loans and mortgage-backed securities held by any bridge depository institution pursuant to section 11(n) of the Federal Deposit Insurance Act; and (C) the Board [of Governors of the Federal Reserve System], with respect to any mortgage or mortgage-backed securities or pool of securities held, owned, or controlled by or on behalf of a Federal reserve bank, other than mortgages or securities held, owned, or controlled in connection with open market operations under section 14 of the Federal Reserve Act (12 U.S.C. 353), or as collateral for an advance or discount that is not in default.

Section 110(b)(5) of EESA requires each federal property manager to submit a report to Congress 60 days after the date of enactment of the act, and every 30 days thereafter, providing "specific information on the number and types of loan modifications made and the number of actual foreclosures occurring during the reporting period in accordance with this section."[15]

Section 116(b) (Financial Statements)

As noted previously in this report, Section 116(b) of the act requires the TARP to "annually prepare and issue to the appropriate committees of Congress and the public audited financial statements prepared in accordance with generally accepted accounting principles." Those financial statements are required to be "on the fiscal year basis prescribed under section 1102 of title 31, United States Code. Section 116(c)(2) requires these audits to "(A) state the responsibility of management for establishing and maintaining adequate internal control over financial reporting; and (B) state its assessment, as of the end of the most recent year covered by such financial statement of the TARP, of the effectiveness of the internal control over financial reporting." Section 116(d) requires this audit to be shared with the COP.

Section 129 (Disclosures on Exercise of Loan Authority)

Section 129(a) of EESA states

> Not later than 7 days after the date on which the Board [of Governors of the Federal Reserve System] exercises its authority under the third paragraph of section 13 of the Federal Reserve Act (12 U.S.C. 343; relating to discounts for individuals, partnerships, and corporations) the Board shall provide to the Committee on Banking, Housing, and Urban Affairs of the Senate and the Committee on Financial Services of the House of Representatives a report which includes (1) the justification for exercising the authority; and (2) the specific terms of the actions of the Board, including the size and duration of the lending, available information concerning the value of any collateral held with respect to such a loan, the recipient of warrants or any other potential equity in exchange for the loan, and any expected cost to the taxpayers for such exercise.[16]

Section 129(b) requires the Board to provide updates to these committees at least every 60 days "while the subject loan is outstanding, including (1) the status of the loan; (2) the value of the collateral held by the Federal Reserve bank which initiated the loan; and (3) the projected cost to the taxpayers of the loan." Section 129(e) requires that these reports also be sent to the COP.

Section 133(b) (Mark-to-Market Accounting)

Section 133(a) requires the Securities and Exchange Commission, in consultation with the Board of Governors of the Federal Reserve System and the Secretary of the Treasury, to "conduct a study on mark-to-market accounting standards as provided in Statement Number 157 of the Financial Accounting Standards Board, as such standards are applicable to financial institutions, including depository institutions." That section also delineates several elements that the study "shall consider," including the effects of such standards on a financial institution's balance sheet, and the impact of such accounting on bank failures in 2008. Section 133(b) requires the Securities and Exchange Commission to "submit to Congress a report of such study before the end of the 90-day period beginning on the date of the enactment of this Act containing the findings and determinations of the Commission, including such administrative and legislative recommendations as the Commission determines appropriate."[17]

CONCLUDING OBSERVATIONS

The preceding review of EESA's reporting requirements indicates that those requirements are both numerous and varied. The entities tasked with submitting EESA reports include (1) the Secretary of the Treasury, (2) the Financial Stability Oversight Board, (3) the COP, (4) the Special Inspector General for the TARP, (5) the Comptroller General, (6) the Director of OMB (and OMB itself), (7) the Congressional Budget Office, (8) federal property managers, (9) the Board of Governors of the Federal Reserve System, and (10) the Securities and Exchange Commission. In one case (Section 116(b)), the reporting requirement is placed on a program (the Troubled Asset Relief Program) rather than an individual or an organization.[18]

The designated recipients of the reports are equally varied, including

- the "appropriate" congressional committees (defined as the Senate Committees on Banking, Housing, and Urban Affairs; Finance; Budget; and Appropriations; and the House Committees on Financial Services, Ways and Means, Budget, and Appropriations;
- a subset of those "appropriate committees" (e.g., in Section 116(b) and Section 117, only the Senate Committee on Banking, Housing, and Urban Affairs; and the House Committee on Financial Services);
- Congress as a whole;
- the COP;
- the Special Inspector General for the TARP;
- the President; and
- the public;

No single entity receives all of the EESA-required reports. Also, it is not readily apparent why some of the reports are filed with the set of "appropriate committees," some to a subset of those committees, and some to Congress as a whole. When reports are required to be submitted to "the Congress," the parliamentarian in each house of Congress (on behalf of the Speaker of the House and the presiding officer of the Senate) decides which officers and committees ultimately receive the reports. Some of the entities designated to produce or receive the reports have not been formally established (e.g., the COP and the Special Inspector General), and it is unclear when they will be established.[19] Therefore, it is currently not clear how those reporting requirements will be satisfied.

Many of the act's reporting requirements seem to address the same or similar issues. For example, Section 105(a) requires the Secretary of the Treasury to report to the "appropriate committees" within 60 days and every 30 days afterward on all "actions taken by the Secretary," including all agreements, transactions, and insurance contracts. Section 105(b) requires the Secretary to report to the same committees on the same transactions within seven days of each \$50 billion in commitments to purchase troubled assets. Section 116 requires the Comptroller General to oversee the activities of the TARP and report on his findings at least every 60 days, which would presumably include TARP-related agreements, transactions, and insurance contracts. Section 121 requires the Special Inspector General to report every quarter on its audits of (among other things) all "troubled assets" purchased or sold under Section 101, and the management of any insurance program under Section 102.

Also, Section 105(c) of the act requires the Secretary of the Treasury to review the current state of the financial markets and the regulatory system and submit a written report to the appropriate committees of Congress not later than April 30, 2009. That report is also required to provide recommendations regarding whether any participants in the financial markets that are currently outside the regulatory system should become subject to the regulatory system. Similarly, Section 125(b)(2) requires the COP to submit a "special report on regulatory reform" by January 20, 2009, "analyzing the current state of the regulatory system and its effectiveness at overseeing the participants in the financial system and protecting consumers." The report is also required to provide "recommendations for improvement, including recommendations regarding whether any participants in the financial markets that are currently outside the regulatory system should become subject to the regulatory system."

The number and variety of the required reports may have been intended to provide a variety of perspectives on the implementation of EESA, but the lack of integration of those requirements may make understanding the implementation of the act difficult. Also, given the nature of the "troubled assets" being purchased under the TARP (i.e., bank stock instead of mortgages or other instruments related to mortgages), it is unclear whether some of the reporting requirements are still relevant to the activities being carried out. For example, Section 105(a)(3) requires the Secretary of the Treasury to provide

> a detailed financial statement with respect to the exercise of authority under this Act, including (A) all agreements made or renewed; (B) all insurance contracts entered into pursuant to section 102; (C) all transactions occurring during such period, including the types of parties involved; (D) the nature of the assets purchased; (E) all projected costs and liabilities; (F) operating expenses, including compensation for financial agents; (G) the valuation or pricing method used for each transaction; and (H) a description of the vehicles established to exercise such authority.

The Secretary of the Treasury announced on November 12 that the Department of the Treasury no longer plans to buy mortgage-based "troubled assets," and will instead "aid banks and other firms that issue student, auto, and credit card loans in part by jump-starting the market that provides financing for these companies."[20] Therefore, some of these particular reporting requirements may no longer be relevant or helpful. As a result, some have called for Congress to revisit EESA's reporting requirements.[21]

Other information that is not specifically required by the act may be more useful to Congress and others as they oversee the implementation of the program. For example, several Members of Congress have expressed concerns that the funds being invested in banks are being used to pay dividends to stockholders, purchase smaller banks, or finance bonuses and other types of compensation for bank executives — not to increase lending.[22] Although some of the reporting requirements appear to be general enough to allow the reporting entities to include how the funds were used, no individual or organization is currently required to do so.

Also, although Section 2(2)(D) of EESA says one of the purposes of the legislation is to provide "public accountability" for the use of the act's authorities, only one of the reports is required by EESA to be made to the public.[23] It is currently unclear whether, and if so, how, the other reports will be made public by either the recipients or the producers of the reports.[24]

Some of the reports are required to be submitted to the recipients relatively quickly, and some of the reporting deadlines appear to have already occurred. For example, the trigger for several of the reports is the first use of the authority provided to the Secretary of the Treasury in Section 101 to purchase troubled assets. The first exercise of section 101(a) authority occurred on October 28, 2008, when the Secretary purchased $125 billion in preferred stock from nine large banks.[25] Therefore, for example

- because Section 105(b)(2) requires the Secretary of the Treasury to submit a report to the "appropriate congressional committees" within seven days after the first $50 billion in troubled assets are purchased, that report appears to have been required by November 4, 2008.
- because Section 125(b)(1)(B) requires that the COP submit a report to Congress "not later than 30 days after the first exercise by the Secretary of the authority under section 101(a) or 102," that report appears to be required by November 27, 2008.
- because Section 110(b)(5) requires each federal property manager to submit a report to Congress 60 days after the enactment of EESA, that report appears to be required by December 2, 2008.
- because Section 202(a) of the act requires OMB to submit a report to the President and Congress within 60 days of the first exercise of the authority granted in section 101(a), the OMB report appears to be required by December 27, 2008.

On the other hand, some of the reports are not required for years. For example, Section 134 of the act requires OMB to "submit a report to the Congress on the net amount within the Troubled Asset Relief Program under this Act" five years after the date that EESA was enacted (i.e., on October 3, 2013). Some of the reporting requirements are recurring (e.g., in Section 125(b)(1), which requires the COP to submit its regular reports every 30 days). Other reports, however, are only required to be submitted one time (e.g., in Section 125(b)(2), which requires the COP to submit a special report to Congress by January 20, 2009).

Appendix. Reporting Requirements in the Emergency Economic Stabilization Act of 2008 (EESA, P.L. 110-343)

EESA Section	Report Prepared by	Report Delivered to	When First Report is Required	Frequency of Reports	When Reports End
102(b) — TARP Report	Secretary of the Treasury	"appropriate committees of Congress"	90 days after Enactment of EESA (i.e., by 01/01/09)	one time	when the report is submitted
105(a) — General Reports	Secretary of the Treasury	"appropriate committees of Congress"	within 60 days after the first exercise of authority under Sections 101(a) and 102	every 30 days after the first report	the date the last troubled asset is sold or transferred, or the expiration of the last insurance contract
105(b) — Tranche Reports	Secretary of the Treasury	"appropriate committees of Congress" and the Congressional Oversight Panel (COP)	within seven days after the purchase of $50 billion in troubled assets	within seven days after each $50 billion interval	seven days after the last purchase of troubled assets
105(c) — Regulatory Report	Secretary of the Treasury	"appropriate committees of Congress" and the COP	by 04/30/09	one time	when the report is submitted

(Continued)

EESA Section	Report Prepared by	Report Delivered to	When First Report is Required	Frequency of Reports	When Reports End
104(g) — Reports on Sections 101 and 102 of EESA	Financial Stability Oversight Board	"appropriate committees of Congress" and the COP	unclear	at least quarterly	unclear, although the Board terminates 15 days after the last troubled asset is sold or transferred, or the expiration of the last inurance contract
125(b)(1) — Regular Reports	COP	Congress	within 30 days after the first exercise of authority under Sections 101(a) and 102	every 30 days after the first report	unclear, although the Panel terminates on or about 06/30/2010
125(b)(2) — Special Report on Regulatory Reform	COP	Congress	by 01/20/09	one time	when the report is submitted
121(f)(1) — Inspector General Report	Special Inspector General	"appropriate comm-ittees of Congress" and the COP	within 60 days after confirmation of the Special Inspector General	every "calendar quarter" after the first report	unclear, but the Off-ice of the Special Inspector General terminates on the later of the date that the last troubled asset is sold or transferred, or the last insurance contract expires

(Continued)

EESA Section	Report Prepared by	Report Delivered to	When First Report is Required	Frequency of Reports	When Reports End
116(a)(3) — Oversight Report	Comptroller General	"appropriate comm-ittees of Congress," the Special Inspector General, and theCOP	unclear	"regularly and no less freque-ntly than once every 60 days"	unclear
116(b) — Audit of TARP Financial State-ment Audit	Comptroller General	sent to the COP, the "appropriate com-mittees of Congr-ess," and the public	unclear	annually	unclear, although the TARP's auth-ority expires 12/31/09
117 — Margin Authority Report	Comptroller General	Senate Committee on Banking, Housing, and Urban Affairs; and the House Com- mittee on Financial Services	By 06/01/09	one time	when the report is submitted
134 — Recoupment Report	Director of the Office of Ma-Nagement and Budget	Congress	Five years after the enactment of EESA (i.e., 10/03/13)	one time	when the report is submitted
202(a) — Cost of TARP	Office of Management and Budget	President and Congress	within 60 days after the first exercise of au-thority under Section 101(a) (i.e., by 12/27/08)	"semi-annually"	unclear

(Continued)

EESA Section	Report Prepared by	Report Delivered to	When First Report is Required	Frequency of Reports	When Reports End
202(b) — Assessment of OMB Report	Congressional Budget Office	Congress	within 45 days after the first report required in Section 202(a)	within 45 days after each "semi annual" report under Section 202(a)	unclear
110(b)(5) — Homeowner Assistance	each "federal property manager"[a]	Congress	60 days after the enactment of EESA (i.e., by 12/03/08)	every 30 days after the first report	unclear
116(b) — Financial Statements	Troubled Asset Relief Program	"appropriate comm.-ittees of Congress" and the public	unclear	annually	unclear, although the TARP's autho-rity expires 12/31/09
129 — Disclosures on Exercise of Loan Authority	Board of Governors of the Federal Reserve System	Senate Committee on Banking, Housing, and Urban Affairs; House Committee on Financial Services; and the COP	within seven days after the Board exercises its authority under the third paragraph of section 13 of the Federal Reserve Act (12 U.S.C. §343)	at least every 60 days	until the loan is no longer outstanding

(Continued)

EESA Section	Report Prepared by	Report Delivered to	When First Report is Required	Frequency of Reports	When Reports End
133 — Mark-to-Market Accounting Report	Securities and Exchange Commission[b]	Congress	within 90 days after the date that EESA is enacted (i.e., by 01/01/09)	one-time	when the report is submitted

Notes: a. Section 110(a)(1) of EESA defines a "federal property manager" as "(A) the Federal Housing Finance Agency, in its capacity as conservator of the Federal National Mortgage Association and the Federal Home Loan Mortgage Corporation; (B) the [Federal Deposit Insurance] Corporation, with respect to residential mortgage loans and mortgage-backed securities held by any bridge depository institution pursuant to section 11(n) of the Federal Deposit Insurance Act; and (C) the Board [of Governors of the Federal Reserve System], with respect to any mortgage or mortgage-backed securities or pool of securities held, owned, or controlled by or on behalf of a Federal reserve bank, other than mortgages or securities held, owned, or controlled in connection with open market operations under section 14 of the Federal Reserve Act (12 U.S.C. 353), or as collateral for an advance or discount that is not in default."

b. The Securities and Exchange Commission is required to consult with the Board of Governors of the Federal Reserve System and the Secretary of the Treasury in the conduct of the study underlying this report.

Most of the reporting requirements include clear starting or ending points for the submission of the reports (e.g., those that are required within 30 days after the date that EESA was enacted, or those that require a report by a certain date). In some cases, however, the starting points for the reporting deadlines are unclear. For example, Section 104(g) requires the Financial Stability Oversight Board to submit reports "not less frequently than quarterly," but the act does not indicate when these reports are to begin. Similarly, Section 116(a)(3) requires the Comptroller General to report "no less frequently than once every 60 days," but does not indicate when those reports are to begin.

Finally, some of the reporting requirements (e.g., those placed on the Secretary by Section 105) expire on the date that the last troubled asset is sold or transferred, or the date that the last insurance contract expires. Without some kind of a lag period for the expiration of these reporting requirements (e.g., 30 or 60 days after the last sale or transfer of troubled assets), a complete history of these transactions may not be provided to Congress or the public.

End Notes

[1] For more information on EESA and related issues, see CRS Report RL34730, *The Emergency Economic Stabilization Act and Current Financial Turmoil: Issues and Analysis*, by Baird Webel and Edward V. Murphy.

[2] The Financial Stability Oversight Board comprises the Chairman of the Board of Governors of the Federal Reserve System, the Secretary of the Treasury, the Director of the Federal Housing Finance Agency, the Chairman of the Securities and Exchange Commission, and the Secretary of Housing and Urban Development.

[3] Members of the COP are appointed as follows: one each by the Speaker of the House of Representatives, the minority leader of the House, the majority leader of the Senate, and the minority leader of the Senate; and one by the Speaker and the majority leader of the Senate, after consultation with the minority leaders in each house.

[4] The Special Inspector General is appointed by the President, by and with the advice and consent of the Senate. For more information on how the Special Inspector General for the TARP compares with other inspectors general, see CRS Report RS22981, *The Special Inspector General for the Troubled Asset Relief Program (SIG TARP)*, by Vanessa K. Burrows.

[5] For more information on the oversight and audit responsibilities established in the act, see CRS Report RL34713, *Emergency Economic Stabilization Act: Preliminary Analysis of Oversight Provisions*, by Curtis W. Copeland.

[6] For more information on EESA's insurance program, see CRS Report RS22969, *The Emergency Economic Stabilization Act's Insurance for Troubled Assets*, by Baird Webel.

[7] Because EESA was enacted on October 3, 2008, this report appears to be required by January 1, 2009.

[8] On October 28, 2008, the Department of the Treasury transferred the first $115 billion of EESA-related funds to participating institutions. See the remarks of Under Secretary for Domestic Finance Anthony Ryan at [http://www.treasury.gov/press/releases/hp1240.htm]. As required, the first of these reports was published on November 4, 2008. See

[http://www.treasury.gov/initiatives/eesa/docs/Tranche-Reportfinal.pdf] for a copy of this report.

[9] On October 28, 2008, the Department of the Treasury transferred the first EESA-related funds to participatinginstitutions. See the remarks of Under Secretary for Domestic Finance Anthony Ryan at [http://www.treasury.gov/press/releases/hp1240.htm]. Therefore, it appears that the first of these reports is required by November 27, 2008.

[10] According to the interim Assistant Secretary of the Treasury, the President is expected to submit a nomination for the Special Inspector General position in November 2008.

[11] Section 116(a) of the act requires the Comptroller General to conduct "ongoing oversight of the activities and performance of the TARP and of any agents and representatives of the TARP (as related to the agent or representative's activities on behalf of or under the authority of the TARP), including vehicles established by the Secretary under this Act." Specific issues delineated in the act include the "characteristics of transactions and commitments entered into," "characteristics and disposition of acquired assets," and "the efforts of the TARP to prevent, identify, and minimize conflicts of interest involving any agent or representative performing activities on behalf of or under the authority of the TARP."

[12] Although it is not required to do so, the TARP may also include GAO's audit in the financial statement that is sent to the "appropriate committees of Congress" and the public.

[13] The first troubled assets were purchased on October 28, 2008. Therefore, this report appears to be required by December 27, 2008.

[14] Because the OMB report appears to be required by December 27, 2008, the CBO report appears to be required by February 10, 2009.

[15] Because EESA was enacted on October 3, 2008, this report appears to be required by December 2, 2008.

[16] Section 13(3) of the Federal Reserve Act, invoked in the Bear Stearns and AIG interventions, authorizes the Federal Reserve Board to lend to any firm or individual in "unusual or exigent circumstances." However, because those actions predated EESA, they did not trigger this reporting requirement. For more information on this issue, see CRS Report RL34427, *Financial Turmoil: Federal Reserve Policy Responses*, by Marc Labonte.

[17] Because EESA was enacted on October 3, 2008, this report appears to be required by January 1, 2009.

[18] In this case, because the TARP is authorized to be established by the Secretary of the Treasury (Section 101(a)(1) of the act), the Secretary or the Office of Financial Stability that is required to implement the program may actually carry out this requirement.

[19] For example, EESA requires the Special Inspector General to be appointed by the President with the advice and consent of the Senate. According to the interim Assistant Secretary, the President is expected to submit a nomination for the position in November 2008. Unless the Senate reconvenes after the nomination is submitted, a Special Inspector General may not be confirmed until the 111th Congress begins in 2009.

[20] Peter Whoriskey, David Cho, and Binyamin Appelbaum, "Treasury Redefines Its Rescue Program," *Washington Post*, p. A1.

[21] See, for example, Alan B. Morrison, "Plugging the Leaks in the Bailout," *Legal Times*, November 10, 2008, p. 46. Specifically, he said "the bill was primarily intended to provide funds to buy up bad mortgage-related securities and to help homeowners, but it was quickly used to make the United States a co-owner of a number of large and probably smaller banks." For that and other reasons, he said, "Congress needs to take another hard look at its handiwork."

[22] See, for example, Binyamin Appelbaum, "Banks to Continue Paying Dividends; Bailout Money Is for Lending, Critics Say," *Washington Post*, October 30, 2008, p. A1; and Charlene Carter, "Leading House Democrats Pressure Treasury on Banks' Use of Federal Funds," *CongressNow*, October 31, 2008.

[23] Section 116(b) of the act requires the TARP to prepare and issue audited financial statements to the appropriate committees of Congress and the public.

[24] As noted earlier in this report, although not required to do so, the first "tranche" report was posted on the Department of the Treasury's public website on November 4, 2008. See [http://www.treasury.gov/initiatives/eesa/docs/Tranche-Reportfinal.pdf] for a copy.

[25] On October 28, 2008, the Department of the Treasury transferred the first EESA-related funds to participating institutions. See the remarks of Under Secretary for Domestic Finance Anthony Ryan at [http://www.treasury.gov/press/releases/hp1240.htm].

In: Emergency Economic Stabilization Act ISBN: 978-1-60741-327-1
Editor: Nikola Vazquez

Chapter 4

"FAST TRACK" PARLIAMENTARY PROCEDURES OF THE EMERGENCY ECONOMIC STABILIZATION ACT*

Christopher M. Davis

SUMMARY

The Emergency Economic Stabilization Act of 2008 (Division A of H.R. 1424, P.L. 110-343) empowers the Secretary of the Treasury to purchase certain "troubled assets" as a means to stabilize the economy. Should the Secretary wish to have more than $350 billion outstanding under the troubled assets program, the President must submit a written report to Congress detailing the Secretary's request and his plan to implement it. The receipt of this report triggers a 15-day period during which Congress may reject the Secretary's request by enacting a joint resolution of disapproval. This disapproval resolution would be considered in the House and Senate under "fast track" parliamentary procedures which are intended to ensure an opportunity to consider and vote on the measure. This report examines these procedures and explains how they differ from the regular parliamentary mechanisms of the House and Senate. It will be updated as needed.[1]

---

* This is an edited, reformatted and augmented version of a CRS Report for Congress, Report RS22985 dated November 14, 2008.

Graduated Authorization to Purchase

The Emergency Economic Stabilization Act of 2008 (EESA)[2] empowers the Secretary of the Treasury to purchase and insure certain "troubled assets" as a means to establish stability in the nation's financial system, and authorizes funds on a graduated scale that the Secretary may use for this purpose. The act immediately authorizes the Secretary to have *up to* $250 billion outstanding at any one time under the troubled assets purchase program. This authorized maximum will automatically increase to $350 billion outstanding upon the President's submission to Congress of a certification of need.

Should the Secretary of the Treasury wish to have *in excess* of $350 billion outstanding at any one time under the troubled asset purchase program, the President must submit a written report to Congress detailing the Secretary's plan to exercise this additional authority. The submission of this report triggers a 15-calendar day period during which Congress may enact a joint resolution disapproving the request. The act further establishes special "fast track" parliamentary procedures for congressional consideration of this joint resolution. Should Congress either choose not to, or be unable to successfully, enact a disapproval resolution by the expiration of this 15-day period, the Secretary's authority would automatically increase up to $700 billion in outstanding purchases at one time under the troubled assets program.

Expedited Parliamentary Procedures

Section 115(c) of EESA establishes a set of expedited parliamentary procedures by which Congress may consider a joint resolution rejecting the Secretary's plan. Statutes that contain provisions establishing expedited procedures regulating the consideration of particular legislation are frequently called "rulemaking statutes," because their procedures have the same force and effect of standing rules of the House or Senate.[3] These expedited legislative procedures were created by Congress to ensure that it could promptly consider and act on the Secretary's proposal within the 15-day time frame. The procedures accomplish this goal by exempting the joint resolution of disapproval from many of the ordinary time-consuming steps and legislative obstacles that apply to most other measures Congress considers. In short, the resolution is considered not under the ordinary parliamentary procedures of the

House and Senate, which are, by design, slow and uncertain, but on a special parliamentary "fast track." These procedures address:

Reconvening Congress

Should Congress receive a report from the President detailing the Secretary of the Treasury's desire to have more than $350 billion outstanding under the troubled assets purchase program, EESA directs the Speaker, if the House has adjourned, to notify Members that the chamber will reconvene not later than the second calendar day thereafter. Likewise, if the Senate has adjourned or recessed for more than two days, the Senate majority leader, after consultation with the minority leader, is to notify Senators that the body will reconvene.

Under modern practice, when one or both chambers adjourn for more than three days, the adjournment resolution adopted by the House and Senate grants its leaders discretionary authority to recall the chambers in the event of an emergency or if the public interest warrants.[4] Interestingly, EESA seems to make Congress's reconvening mandatory— even if one or both chambers does not wish to disapprove the plan.

Text of the Joint Resolution

Unlike bills, joint resolutions often include a preamble.[5] The joint resolution of disapproval under EESA, however, may not contain a preamble. The title of the joint resolution is specified by the statute: *"Joint resolution relating to the disapproval of obligations under the Emergency Economic Stabilization Act of 2008."* Its text is mandated as well: "*That Congress disapproves the obligation of any amount exceeding the amounts obligated as described in paragraphs (1) and (2) of section 115(a) of the Emergency Economic Stabilization Act of 2008."* It is arguably necessary for the statute to specify the precise text of the joint resolution because, unless it is clear which measure Congress intends to be considered under expedited terms, unrelated measures or provisions might "hitch a ride" on the special parliamentary privilege that is afforded the joint resolution, shortcutting the regular legislative process and the rights of all Members.

Introduction

In the regular order of business, a Member of Congress may introduce legislation at any time their chamber is in session during the two-year Congress. EESA, however, establishes a far narrower window in which Members may introduce a qualifying joint resolution of disapproval. In order to qualify for the expedited procedures outlined in the act, a joint disapproval resolution must be introduced not later than three calendar days after the date on which the President's report detailing the Secretary's plan is received by Congress. Although the statute is silent on the question, joint resolutions may conceivably be introduced by any Member in either chamber. Because the mandatory recall provisions described above, however, make it possible that the House or Senate may not reconvene until two calendar days after the report's submission, it is possible (even likely) that Members will have only a single calendar day in which to introduce a qualifying joint resolution of disapproval.

Referral to Committee

EESA is silent on the referral process for a joint resolution of disapproval introduced in the House of Representatives, and the Speaker would presumably refer the measure to committee in keeping with regular practice and her authority under chamber rules. In the Senate, when a joint resolution is introduced, under the terms of EESA, it is not referred to committee at all, but is instead placed directly on the Senate Calendar of Business. Under normal Senate practice, when legislation is introduced, it is referred to committee based on the subject matter that predominates in it. Under Senate Rule XIV, a measure might be placed directly on the Senate Calendar of Business upon introduction via a process of objecting to the first two readings of the measure, which technically must occur on different legislative days. Under EESA, referring the joint resolution to Senate committee, rather than placing it directly on the calendar, would seem to require unanimous consent.

Committee Action in the House

With certain exceptions — for example, when time limits are placed on the sequential referral of a bill by the Speaker of the House — Congress generally does not mandate that a legislative committee act on legislation referred to it within a specified time frame or at all. The EESA expedited procedure, however, requires a committee of referral to act and creates parliamentary mechanisms to take the resolution away from it should it fail to do so.

Under EESA, if a House committee has not reported the joint resolution of disapproval within five days after Congress's receipt of the President's report, the committee is automatically discharged from its further consideration and the measure is placed directly on the appropriate calendar. These expediting provisions theoretically make it impossible for a joint resolution of disapproval to be long delayed or killed outright by the inaction of a legislative committee. The statute is silent on whether a committee may amend the resolution, but because (as has been noted) the precise text of the joint resolution is specified by the act, any attempt to alter it by amendment would likely be interpreted as destroying the special parliamentarystatus it enjoys. Additionally, because the procedure precludes the consideration of amendments to the joint resolution on the House floor (discussed below), committee amendments would also be barred. A House committee would presumably still have the option of reporting a measure to the chamber favorably, adversely, or without recommendation.

Calling Up the Joint Resolution on the Floor

After each House committee of referral has reported or been discharged from the further consideration of the joint resolution, it is in order, not later than the sixth calendar day following the submission of the President's report, for any Member to make a non-debatable motion to proceed to its consideration. Such a motion cannot be repeated after one has already been disposed of, and the vote on the motion may not be reconsidered.

In the Senate, under most circumstances, a motion to proceed to the consideration of a measure is fully debatable.[6] The motion to proceed to the consideration of the joint resolution of disapproval under EESA, however, is not debatable or amendable, and it cannot be postponed. The motion is in order in the Senate at any time during the period beginning on the fourth day after the date on which Congress receives the President's report and ending on the sixth day after receipt. In the Senate, the motion to proceed is permitted even if a previous motion to the same effect has been defeated. If a motion to proceed is agreed to, the chamber immediately proceeds to consider the joint resolution without intervening motion, order, or business. Having chosen to take up the disapproval resolution by adopting the motion to proceed, consideration of the measure is, in a sense, "locked in." The joint resolution remains the unfinished business of the chamber until the chamber disposes of it.

Floor Debate

In the absence of a special rule dictating otherwise, the House of Representatives ordinarily debates measures under the one hour rule or under other procedures which establish specific periods for debate, such as the suspension of the rules procedure. In keeping with its expediting nature, EESA limits the amount of time for House floor consideration of the joint resolution of disapproval. Debate in the House on the joint resolution, and all debatable motions and appeals connected with it, is limited to not more than two hours, equally divided between a proponent and an opponent.

In the Senate, debate is ordinarily unlimited unless it has been structured by unanimous consent or limited by the invocation of cloture under Senate Rule XXII. Under EESA, however, Senate debate on the joint disapproval resolution, and on all debatable motions and appeals in connection therewith, is limited to not more than 10 hours, divided equally between the majority and minority leaders or their designees. A non-debatable motion to further limit debate is in order. Using this device, the Senate could, by majority vote, reduce debate time below 10 hours.

Motions, Amendments, Voting

EESA includes provisions which make it difficult to delay or set the joint resolution aside without a vote, for example, by returning it to legislative committee or the calendar. Amendments to the joint resolution of disapproval are not in order in either chamber. In the House, all points of order against the joint resolution and its consideration are waived, and the previous question is considered to be ordered to its final passage without any intervening motion, including a motion to recommit. Thus, at the conclusion of debate, the House would automatically vote on adoption of the measure.

In the Senate, the joint resolution is not subject to a motion to postpone, to recommit, or a motion to proceed to the consideration of other business. A motion to reconsider the vote by which the joint resolution is agreed to or disagreed to is also not in order. After the conclusion of debate and a single quorum call (if requested), the chamber immediately would vote on final passage of the joint resolution. Appeals from the decision of the chair relating to consideration of the joint resolution are to be decided without debate.

Automatic Legislative "Hookup"

The EESA also includes provisions to facilitate the exchange of legislation between the House and Senate. If, before voting upon its own joint resolution, a chamber receives a joint resolution passed by the other chamber, that engrossed joint resolution is not referred to committee. The second chamber will proceed to consider its own joint resolution in the fashion laid out in the statute, until the point of final disposition, when the vote taken will be on the engrossed resolution passed by the first chamber. The purpose of this provision is to avoid the need to expend time choosing whether ultimately to act upon the House or Senate vehicle.

Additional Provisions

EESA includes a number of additional provisions intended to expedite consideration of the joint resolution of disapproval. For example, if one chamber fails to introduce or consider a joint resolution under EESA, the resolution of the other House is entitled to "fast track" consideration in the other chamber. If, following passage of the joint resolution in the Senate, it then receives a companion measure from the House, that companion measure is not debatable.

EESA includes provisions stating that if Congress passes a joint resolution, the period beginning on the date the President is presented with the enrolled joint resolution, and ending on the date he takes action on it, is disregarded in computing the 15-calendar day period before an increase in the Secretary's authorization automatically goes into effect. Likewise, if the President vetoes the measure, the period beginning on the date of the veto, and ending on the date Congress receives the veto message, is not calculated. These provisions are included to ensure that the President cannot simply "run out" the 15day time clock once the joint resolution is presented to him for signature.

Finally, in the event of a Presidential veto, debate on a veto message in the Senate is limited to one hour equally divided between the majority and minority leaders or their designees. Under ordinary circumstances, such a veto message would be fully debatable. The act is silent on House consideration of a veto message.

Implications of Resolutions of Disapproval

Under the terms of EESA, a joint resolution must be enacted in order to disapprove the Treasury Secretary's plan. This means that not only would it have to pass both chambers, but it must also be signed by the President, or enacted over his veto, to take effect. For this reason, some Members have argued that resolutions of disapproval of this type generally put Congress at an institutional disadvantage relative to the Executive, in that a President is almost certain to veto the resolution. During debate over the enactment of a different rulemaking statute which included a joint disapproval resolution, one Member voiced this view of the power relationship between the branches, stating,

> A veto would, of course, be likely since the resolution would be disapproving what the executive has proposed. Then it would take two-thirds majorities in both Houses of Congress to effectuate the Congress' expression of disapproval. In other words, a resolution of disapproval would allow as few as 34 Senators, working with one Chief Executive, to block the will of ... Members of Congress.[7]

Conversely, others have argued that resolutions of disapproval give the President necessary flexibility to act, while still reserving the prerogative of Congress to overrule him and influence important policy questions.

Either Chamber May Alter the Expedited Procedure

The fact that an expedited procedure like that of EESA is contained in a rulemaking statute does not mean that another law must be passed in order to alter it. It is sufficient that a majority of Members of either chamber agree to ignore or alter the expedited procedure in order to change the way in which its features apply in that chamber at a given time. Because Article I, Section 5 of the Constitution gives each chamber of Congress the power to determine the rules of its proceedings, expedited procedure statutes like those contained in EESA can (like all rules of the House or Senate) be set aside, altered, or amended by either chamber at any time.[8] These changes can be accomplished by the House through the adoption of a special rule reported by Committee on Rules, by suspension of the rules, or by unanimous consent. In fact, prior practice suggests that the House of Representatives routinely supplants the terms of rulemaking statutes by adopting special rules by majority vote.

Although the same Constitutional authority to determine its own rules resides equally in both houses of Congress, expedited procedures are, in a sense, more binding on the Senate than they are on the House. The Senate operates largely under terms achieved by the unanimous consent of all Senators. If that consent can not be achieved, altering an established rulemaking statute would, in all likelihood, require either the 3/5ths of Senators chosen and sworn (60 if there are no vacancies)[9] necessary to invoke cloture or the concurrence of two-thirds present and voting (67 if all Senators vote) necessary to suspend the rules. Motions to suspend the rules also require written notice one calendar day in advance, and are fully debatable.

End Notes

[1] For information on the policy questions relating to this law, see CRS Report RL34730, *The Emergency Economic Stabilization Act and Current Financial Turmoil: Issues and Analysis,* by Baird Webel and Edward V. Murphy.

[2] P.L. 110-343. 122 Stat. 3831.

[3] CRS Report RS20234, *Expedited or "Fast-Track" Legislative Procedures*, by Christopher M. Davis.

[4] William Holmes Brown, Charles W. Johnson, *House Practice, A Guide to the Rules, Precedents, and Procedures of the House*, 108th Cong., 1st sess. (Washington: GPO, 2003), ch.1, §10, pp. 9-10.

[5] Ibid., ch.6, §5, p. 171.

[6] The motion to proceed to consider conference reports, nominations, treaties, and legislation under certain rulemaking statutes is not debatable. The motion is also not debatable when made during the Morning Hour.

[7] Rep. Jack B. Brooks, remarks in the House, *Congressional Record*, vol. 134, July 7, 1988, p. 17080.

[8] William Holmes Brown and Charles W. Johnson, *House Practice,* ch.50, §4, p. 826.

[9] Under Senate precedents, amending a *statutory* rule does not trigger the prior notice or higher threshold to invoke cloture required for amendments to the chamber's *standing* rules. See *Congressional Record*, vol. 131, July 25, 1985, pp. 20447-20448.

In: Emergency Economic Stabilization Act
Editor: Nikola Vazquez
ISBN: 978-1-60741-327-1

Chapter 5

THE EMERGENCY ECONOMIC STABILIZATION ACT'S INSURANCE FOR TROUBLED ASSETS*

Baird Webel

SUMMARY

Many observers trace the root cause of recent instability in financial markets to uncertainty surrounding the value of widely held securities that are based on mortgages and mortgage-related assets. Losses on these securities have led to the unexpected and relatively sudden failure of several large financial institutions. Credit markets have nearly frozen at times as financial institutions demanded very high interest rates on traditionally routine short-term lending. While there is limited evidence that financial turmoil has caused widespread damage in the broader economy, it is feared that significant real economic effects may be forthcoming, particularly if credit markets remain frozen.

Responding to these economic fears, the House took up the Emergency Economic Stabilization Act of 2008 (EESA) as an amendment to H.R. 3997 on September 29, 2008. This amendment failed by a vote of 205-228. Following this, the Senate took up a bill of the same title with a number of additions and

* This is an edited, reformatted and augmented version of a CRS Report for Congress, Report RS22969 dated October 10, 2008.

passed it by a vote of 74-25 on October 1, 2008, as an amendment to H.R. 1424. On October 3, 2008, the House passed the amended version of H.R. 1424 by a vote of 263-171. The President signed the bill into law, P.L. 110-343, on the same day. Both versions of the act intend to address recent instability in the financial market through a variety of measures, including an insurance program for "troubled assets." This insurance program would provide U.S. government guarantees for some of the securities that are perceived as being at the root of the current financial instability. This report briefly summarizes and analyzes the insurance program contained in the enacted version of the EESA; it will be updated as warranted by legislative and market events.

INTRODUCTION

Over the past two decades, mortgages have increasingly been funded indirectly through asset-backed securities and non-bank lenders, rather than directly through deposits in the traditional banking model. In most cases, once a mortgage was made, the mortgage was sold by the entity that originated the loan to another institution, which pooled a large number of these loans together. From this pool of loans, the institution then issued securities whose returns were based on the payments made on the underlying mortgages in the pool. For a variety of market and regulatory reasons, these mortgage-backed securities (MBS) became widely held by nearly every financial institution in the United States and in many institutions worldwide. In addition to the securities directly backed by mortgages, financial institutions created numerous other complex securities and derivatives based on the initial MBS. These secondary products, such as collateralized debt obligations (CDO) and credit default swaps (CDS) were also very widely held.

In 2006 and 2007, the rates of default and non-payment by mortgages holders increased significantly. This, in turn, caused the securities and derivatives ultimately based on these mortgages to lose value. In some cases, securities thought to be safe were completely wiped out. These losses have rippled through the financial system, causing problems for institutions in a number of unexpected ways as well as stress to the general financial system. The failure of large financial institutions including Bear Stearns, IndyMac, Lehman Brothers, AIG, and Wachovia was largely due to this turmoil. Due largely to the uncertainty about what future mortgage default rates will be, as well as who is currently holding MBS, financial markets have nearly frozen at various points in time since August 2007. On September 19, 2008, the Secretary of the Treasury called for a broad program of financial intervention to stabilize markets. The Treasury proposal called for government purchases of up to $700 billion in mortgage-related securities, in the hope that, by partially purging the system of these troubled assets, normal functioning of the financial markets could be restored.

The idea of broad asset purchases, as in the Treasury plan, is only one of a number of methods that could be used to address the uncertainties regarding mortgage-related assets. Among the other concepts put forward in Congress has been that of a federal guarantee program to insure mortgage-related assets. Insurance on municipal securities has been issued by private insurers since the 1970s, and in the past decade many insurers broadened their insurance offerings to include mortgage-related securities. Most of the insurers specializing in this type of insurance have suffered major losses and ratings agency downgrades in the last year.

As a legislative proposal, a federal insurance program for "troubled assets" appeared in the Emergency Economic Stabilization Act of 2008 (EESA), a House amendment to H.R. 3997, which failed in the House on a vote of 205-228 on September 29, 2008. Another version of the EESA, which included the original EESA plus several other provisions not in the first bill,[1] was offered on October 1 in the Senate as an amendment to the previously passed H.R. 1424. The amended version of H.R. 1424 was approved by a Senate vote of 74-25; it was then taken up by the House and passed by a vote of 263171 on October 3, 2008. The President signed the amended version of H.R. 1414, now P.L. 110-343, the same day as House passage.

Federal Insurance of Troubled Assets

Section 102 of P.L. 110-343 provides that if the Secretary of the Treasury creates a program to purchase troubled assets (as authorized in Section 101), he or she shall also create a program to guarantee troubled assets. Troubled assets under the bill are defined as "residential or commercial mortgages and any securities, obligations, or other instruments that are based on or related to such mortgages."[2] The underlying mortgages in question must have been originated before March 14, 2008. The bill also gives the Secretary of the Treasury, after consultation with the Chairman of the Federal Reserve, the authority to purchase any other financial instrument necessary to promote market stability. Congress must be notified of such a purchase, but explicit approval from Congress is not needed.

Aside from the requirement to establish the program, the Secretary of the Treasury has relatively broad authority as to the structure of the program. He or she may not guarantee the prompt payment of more than 100% of the insured securities' interest and principal payments — 100% is typical of bond insurance in the private sector — but the Secretary is free to guarantee less than 100% as well. Aggregate premiums for the insurance are required to cover the expected losses from the insurance program, and the Secretary has the authority to base individual premiums on the risk of the security to be covered, but there is no requirement that premiums be risk-based. The combined size of the purchase and insurance programs for troubled assets authorized in the bill is limited to $700 billion, but the Secretary of the Treasury is free to decide what percentage of the overall amount the two programs occupy.

IMPACT OF THE PROPOSED PROGRAM

Given the authority that the Secretary has to shape the program, along with the host of other uncertainties in the current financial climate, it is difficult to assess the potential impact of the federal guarantee program. In theory, such a program could have a significant impact by improving confidence in the financial markets. In previous market experience with private bond insurance, once a security was guaranteed, it was generally treated as a security with the same credit rating as the insurer. Thus, for example, a single A rated municipal sewer authority could issue a bond that would be treated as AAA if the bond was then insured by a AAA-rated insurer. If the federal government were to issue a 100% guarantee on a mortgage-backed security, even one backed by subprime loans with a high default rate, the market may treat it essentially as a U.S. Treasury security, which is widely considered to be the safest and most liquid security that can be held.[3] If this occurred for a wide swath of the MBS that are currently illiquid and looked at with great skepticism by the markets, theory would suggest that it would restore the confidence that has been absent in the financial markets in recent weeks.

While the asset purchase plan also contained in P.L. 110-343 could provide the same widespread boost to market confidence, an insurance program may have advantages compared with the purchase plan. The insurance plan would result in little or no government ownership of assets with the attendant questions of how these assets are then to be disposed of. The insurance plan, as structured, would be self-financing. There are no provisions in the plan for the outlay of taxpayer monies. An insurance program would also avoid accounting problems that could emerge if the purchasing plan results in asset sales at significant discounts to previous prices. Under mark-to-market accounting rules such asset sales may trigger accounting losses in other companies holding similar securities and might even threaten the solvency of other financial institutions. Such hoped for benefits of the insurance program, however, may also be offset to some degree by practical questions concerning how the plan might actually work. Many of these questions revolve around the overall cost of the insurance program and the individual premiums to be charged for the government guarantee.

Providing guarantees for MBS has, in practice, proved a very risky and costly business over the past year. Most of the bond insurance companies, if they have been able to remain solvent, have seen their stock prices collapse and their credit ratings downgraded as losses have mounted on guarantees for MBS. The primary new entrant to insuring bonds, a subsidiary of Berkshire Hathaway, has specifically indicated it will not insure such securities.[4] It is unclear if and how a federal insurance program would be able to incur fewer losses than private insurers. If the goal of the program is to improve the functioning of the financial system by removing the impediments posed by troubled assets, some would argue the program would not be functioning as intended if the securities it guaranteed were not suffering losses. Some losses may be avoided by insuring the mortgage-related securities at less than 100% value, as specifically authorized in the act. The recent history on mortgage default rates, however, suggests that any significant guarantee program on mortgage-related securities might incur significant losses.

The program established in P.L. 110-343 specifies that the losses from the guarantee program will be covered by the aggregate premiums paid by financial institutions holding the guaranteed securities. This brings up the most critical point in any insurance endeavor whether public or private, namely determining the premiums to be charged for the coverage provided. If the overall premiums are set too low, the endeavor will ultimately fail as the money coming in will not cover the money going out. If the overall premiums are set too high, in this case, fewer mortgage-related securities would be insured than would be possible. This would presumably be counter to the act's goal of restoring liquidity and stability to the U. S. financial system. Setting optimal premiums for mortgage-related securities would require an accurate estimate of what mortgage default rates will be around the country in the future and how these default rates will affect the payment streams on mortgage-related securities. The inability to make such accurate estimates is identified by many to be at the heart of the uncertainty bedeviling the financial system today.

In addition to the question of setting overall premiums so the program remains solvent, the question of setting individual premiums for specific securities is also challenging. The bill includes the authority, but not requirement, to vary premiums "according to the credit risk associated with the particular troubled asset that is being guaranteed." If individual premiums are not risk-based, then the program may suffer from adverse selection, meaning that the program will attract primarily securities that are relatively high risk. If these high risk securities result in higher losses than anticipated, the overall premiums would ultimately have to be raised to keep the program solvent. Higher premiums would likely result in fewer institutions participating in the program and the remaining guaranteed securities being on the whole higher risk than before. If individual premiums are to be risk-based, the insurance will encounter the problems mentioned above with regard to estimating future mortgage default rates. Indeed the difficulties in estimating the impact on individual securities, and thus establishing individual risk-based premiums, would be much greater than simply estimating the overall amount of premiums needed for the program to remain solvent.

CONCLUSION

Many argue that a central driver of the recent turmoil in financial markets has been uncertainty and fear regarding mortgage-related securities that are widely held in the financial system. Among the mechanisms recently passed by Congress to address these problems is a federal program to insure troubled assets. Private insurance to enhance the credit-worthiness and attractiveness of securities has operated for more than 30 years. This record shows that an insurance mechanism can have a role to play in the securities marketplace. Recent private experience insuring mortgage-related assets, however, has been negative; such insurers have experienced large losses and many have faced difficulties remaining solvent. The Department of the Treasury will face significant practical challenges as it implements the federal program to insure troubled assets. Particular difficulties include ensuring the overall solvency of the program through sufficient aggregate premiums and setting individual premiums commensurate with the risks posed by mortgage-related securities.

End Notes

[1] Additional provisions included a temporary increase in the limit on FDIC-provided depository insurance as well as extensive tax provisions that had previously been considered by one or both Houses of Congress.

[2] P.L. 110-343, Section 3.

[3] There is potentially an important difference between Treasury securities and securities that might be guaranteed under this insurance program. Treasury securities are clearly backed by the "full faith and credit" of the U.S. government, and are paid for out of the general taxing authority of the federal government. Under P.L. 110-343, claims on the troubled asset insurance program are to be paid for out of the premiums collected. There is no explicit authority for the program to borrow from the Treasury as with other federal insurance programs, such as flood insurance. If the claims exceed the funds collected through premiums, it is unclear how these claims would be paid.

[4] See CRS Report RL34364, *Bond Insurers: Issues for the 110th Congress*, by Baird Webel and Darryl E. Getter.

In: Emergency Economic Stabilization Act
Editor: Nikola Vazquez
ISBN: 978-1-60741-327-1

Chapter 6

THE SPECIAL INSPECTOR GENERAL FOR THE TROUBLED ASSET RELIEF PROGRAM (SIG TARP)*

Vanessa K. Burrows

SUMMARY

This report discusses the Special Inspector General provisions in the Emergency Economic Stabilization Act of 2008, H.R. 1424, which was enacted as P .L. 110-343 on October 3, 2008. This Act created a Special Inspector General (SIG) for the Troubled Asset Relief Program (TARP). This report will compare the duties and authorities of the SIG TARP to those of the Special Inspector General for Iraq Reconstruction (SIGIR) and the Special Inspector General for Afghanistan Reconstruction (SIGAR), as well as statutory IGs under the Inspector General Act of 1978, as amended (IG Act).

Congress has established statutory offices of inspectors general (IGs) in many executive and legislative branch agencies, as well as two special IGs for programs and operations funded with amounts appropriated for the reconstruction of Iraq and Afghanistan.[1] The four principal responsibilities of IGs are: (1) conducting and supervising audits and investigations; (2) providing coordination and recommending policies for activities designed to promote

* This is an edited, reformatted and augmented version of a CRS Report for Congress, Report RS22981 dated November 5, 2008.

economy and efficiency in agency programs and operations; (3) preventing and detecting fraud, waste, and abuse; and (4) keeping the agency head and Congress fully and currently informed about problems and deficiencies relating to such programs and recommending corrective actions.[2] P.L. 110-343 established an additional special IG for the Troubled Asset Relief Program (SIG TARP), which will address the purchase and insurance of troubled assets.

The provisions in P.L. 110-343 establishing the SIG TARP are similar to the IG provisions for SIGIR and SIGAR in many respects. However, there are important substantive distinctions between these three IGs, which this report will refer to collectively as the "special IGs," as well as between the SIG TARP and statutory IGs created under the IG Act.[3] Due to the ambiguous nature of the statutory language in P.L. 110-343, the scope of the powers and authorities of the SIG TARP is not clear, as discussed below.

Appointment and Removal

The SIG TARP will be a presidentially appointed and Senate confirmed IG, selected "on the basis of integrity and demonstrated ability in accounting, auditing, financial analysis, law, management analysis, public administration, or investigations."[4] Unlike statutory IGs under § 3 of the IG Act, who are also presidentially appointed and Senate confirmed, there is no provision in P.L. 110-343 that requires the SIG TARP to be appointed "without regard to political affiliation and solely" on the basis of the skills listed above. Although the absence of the additional IG Act language regarding political affiliation and appointment based only on job qualification skills does not change the legal protections that the IG Act and P.L. 110-343 afford to the SIG TARP, the SIG TARP may be less independent than other IGs as a practical matter, given that the SIG TARP is not subject to the same appointment constraints.

The nomination of a SIG TARP is required "as soon as practicable" after the establishment of the TARP and the Troubled Assets Insurance Financing Fund.[5] Like other presidentially appointed and Senate-confirmed IGs, the SIG TARP can be removed only by the President, and the President must notify Congress of the reasons for the IG's removal.[6] The President's reasons need not be given in writing and no time limit is set.

Supervision

Unlike IGs in other agencies, who "shall report to and be under the general supervision" of the agency head,[7] the SIG TARP will not be required to report to, or be supervised by, the head of any agency, including the Secretary of the Treasury. The IG Act does not explicitly define the meaning of "general supervision" and its legislative history does not appear to address the scope of the agency head's supervisory role. A court case relying on the legislative history of the IG Act described the agency head's supervisory authority over the IG as "nominal."[8] Instead, under one interpretation of the SIG TARP's duties and responsibilities, discussed below, the SIG TARP will report only to Congress and not the agency head, as specified in § 121(f)(1). This reporting arrangement would be unique among statutory IGs. Additionally, the SIG TARP will have complete discretion in pursuing audits and investigations, and in issuing subpoenas.[9] The absence of such supervision provisions does not mean that the TARP itself will be without an administrator — the Treasury Secretary will be responsible for implementing the TARP through a newly created Office of Financial Stability.[10]

The SIG TARP appears to possess greater latitude in pursuing audits and investigations than the Treasury IG, as the Treasury IG is one of six IGs that may be prevented by an agency head from initiating, carrying out, or completing an audit or investigation, or from issuing a subpoena, for specified reasons such as preventing disclosure of national security matters.[11]

In contrast to the SIG TARP, the other special IGs report to, and are supervised by, the Secretary of State and the Secretary of Defense. SIGIR and SIGAR are also required to keep the Secretaries of State and Defense "fully and currently informed about problems and deficiencies" in program administration and the need for and progress on corrective action.[12] Additionally, SIGIR and SIGAR must coordinate with the IGs for the Departments of State and Defense, and the United States Agency for International Development IG "in carrying out the duties, responsibilities, and authorities of the Inspector General." The provisions for the SIG TARP do not require coordination with the Treasury IG or other IGs.

Duties and Responsibilities

Section 121(c)(3) of P.L. 110-343 provides that the SIG TARP "shall also have the duties and responsibilities of inspectors general under the Inspector

General Act of 1978." On one hand, this provision could mean that the SIG TARP would be responsible for all of the IG duties outlined in the IG Act, presumably as amended, even those that reference interaction with the head of an establishment or those that reference responsibilities not specifically delineated in P.L. 110-343. However, it appears more likely that § 121(c)(3)'s reference to duties and responsibilities may be limited to those under § 4 of the IG Act, which is entitled "Duties and responsibilities; report of criminal violations to Attorney General."

The provision that grants the SIG TARP the same duties and responsibilities as those of IGs under the IG Act also appears in the acts that created SIGIR and SIGAR. This provision seems to bridge some, but not all, of the differences between the authorities of the special IGs and IGs created under the IG Act. If interpreted broadly, this provision will likely encompass the powers, duties, and responsibilities in certain sections of the IG Act, including, but not limited to

§§ 4(a)(2) - (a)(5), which encompass general IG duties and the responsibility to "keep the head of such establishment and the Congress fully and currently informed, by means of the reports required by section 5 and otherwise, concerning fraud and other serious problems, abuses, and deficiencies relating to the administration of programs and operations"; and

§ 4(d), which requires IGs to report expeditiously to the Attorney General when there exist "reasonable grounds to believe there has been a violation of Federal criminal law."

The "and otherwise" language in the requirement that IGs keep Congress "fully and currently informed" has come to be understood in practice to include testiying at congressional hearings, direct communications with Members and staff, various selective or specialized reporting techniques, and responses to congressional inquiries for information, audits, and reports (both verbal and written).

Depending on how § 121(c)(3) is interpreted, it is possible that the SIG TARP's responsibilities will not encompass § 4(a)(1) of the IG Act. That section provides that IGs are "to provide policy direction for and to conduct, supervise, and coordinate audits and investigations relating to the programs and operations of such establishment." Since the provisions creating the SIG TARP contain specific language with regard to conducting, supervising, and coordinating audits and investigations, and this specific language does not mention "policy direction," this provision of the IG Act would not seem to be included in the duties mentioned in § 121(c)(3).

Also, § 121(c)(3) of P.L. 110-343 will not necessarily encompass the whistleblower protections in § 7 of the IG Act. These provisions address complaints or information provided by a whistleblowing employee, the disclosure of a whistleblower's identity, and reprisals threatened or taken against a whistleblower. Under the IG Act, not every complaint must be investigated, and the IG has discretion in accepting complaints from individuals other than employees. However, it appears that IGs are willing to accept complaints from anyone, not just employees, and the legislative history of the IG Act does not prohibit IGs from receiving and acting on information or complaints from any source. On a related note, P.L. 110-343 provides that the Financial Stability Oversight Board, as established by the legislation, will be responsible for "reporting any suspected fraud, misrepresentation, or malfeasance" to the SIG TARP or the Attorney General.[13]

However, a whistleblower with information concerning the possible existence of illegal activities or mismanagement regarding the purchase or insurance of troubled assets could conceivably be covered by the IG Act § 7 protections if he or she reported the information to the Treasury IG, as opposed to the SIG TARP. The acts that created SIGIR and SIGAR do not contain whistleblower protections either.

SIG TARP Reports

If the SIG TARP's duties and responsibilities are interpreted to be confined to those in § 4 of the IG Act, the above cross reference to "the reports required by section 5" in § 4(a)(5) of the IG Act appears to subject the SIG TARP to the IG Act § 5 reporting requirements as well. However, it is not clear as to whether the SIG TARP would need to submit the reports in § 5 of the IG Act in addition to the reports required in P.L. 110-343 or whether the SIG TARP would only be responsible for the required reports set forth in P.L. 110-343.

For example, § 5(d) of the IG Act requires establishment IGs to immediately report "particularly serious or flagrant problems, abuses, or deficiencies" to the head of the establishment whenever the IG becomes aware of such issues. The head of the establishment then must send the report to the appropriate congressional committees within seven days, along with the establishment head's comments in his or her own report. Since P.L. 110-343 requires the SIG TARP to report to Congress only, and not to an establishment head, it is not clear if the SIG TARP would be required to comply with those reporting requirements in § 5(d) of the IG Act. If P.L. 110-343 is interpreted to include the reporting requirements in § 5 of the IG Act, then the SIG TARP could be required to submit certain reports to the establishment head, which would appear to be the Secretary of the Treasury, as TARP itself has not been designated an establishment.

Section 121(f) of P.L. 110-343 specifies certain reporting requirements for the SIG TARP, including a report 60 days after the SIG's confirmation by the Senate and every quarter thereafter. The report must include "a detailed statement of all purchases, obligations, expenditures, and revenues associated with" the TARP. The specificity of the language of this report provision could be interpreted to imply that the "duties and responsibilities" provision in § 121(c)(3) would not extend to the reporting requirements set out in § 5 of the IG Act, which provides that the IG office must prepare semiannual reports and submit them to the head of the establishment, who in turn must transmit them to appropriate congressional committees with his or her own report.[14] Alternatively, the IG Act § 5 reports could be required in addition to the reports set out in P.L. 110-343.

There is no explicit requirement in P.L. 110-343 that the Treasury Secretary (or anyone else) be allowed to comment on the reports that the SIG TARP submits to Congress. Although there may be other reporting requirements with respect to TARP, they would not be intended to respond to SIG concerns or criticisms. SIGAR and SIGIR have such requirements enabling the Secretaries of State and Defense to submit comments to the appropriate congressional committees, as well as requirements that the reports be made public, and even published on a website.[15] The IG Act also provides that the head of the establishment must make the semiannual IG reports and the semiannual establishment head reports available to the public, on request, within 60 days of the establishment head's transmission of the reports to the appropriate congressional committees.[16]

Resources

Section 121(d) of P.L. 110-343 states that the SIG TARP will have the authorities of § 6 of the IG Act, which provides in subsection (c) that the head of an establishment must give the IG office within the establishment adequate office space, equipment, supplies, and other services. It could be argued that the Secretary of the Treasury is the head of the establishment in which the TARP is located, as § 11(2) of the IG Act defines "establishment" to include the Treasury. In addition, § 6(a)(3) of the IG Act provides that the IG is authorized "to request information or assistance as may be necessary for carrying out the duties and responsibilities provided by the IG Act from any Federal, State, or local government agency or unit thereof." It is not clear if "assistance" would cover office space, however, if it does, the SIG TARP would appear to be able to request facilities and resources from the Treasury Department. In contrast, P.L. 110-343 specifically provides that "[t]he Secretary shall provide the Comptroller General with appropriate space and facilities in the Department of the Treasury as necessary to facilitate oversight of the TARP until the termination date established in section 120."[17]

The provisions in the act creating SIGAR enabled that special IG to rely on the personnel, facilities, and resources of another special IG, SIGIR.[18] SIGIR, in turn, could rely on the Department of State or the Department of Defense for equipment, office supplies, and communications facilities and services within either agency, including at appropriate locations of the Department of State in Iraq.[19]

Termination

Section 121(h) establishes that the office of the SIG TARP "shall terminate on the later of — (1) the date that the last troubled asset acquired by the Secretary under section 101 has been sold or transferred out of ownership or control of the Federal Government; or (2) the date of expiration of the last insurance contract issued under section 102."[20] In contrast, SIGIR and SIGAR "shall terminate 180 days after the date on which amounts appropriated or otherwise made available for the reconstruction of Iraq [or Afghanistan] that are unexpended are less than $250,000,000."[21] The continuation of the SIG TARP appears fundamentally different than that of the other special IGs, as the reconstruction of Iraq and Afghanistan accounts are expected to be limited in time and amount. The SIG TARP may be a continuing necessity to audit the purchase, transfer, sale, and insurance of troubled assets.

End Notes

[1] Provisions establishing SIGIR and SIGAR are located at 5 U.S.C. App. § 8G note. Provisions establishing statutory IGs are codified at 5 U.S.C. App.

[2] 5 U.S.C. App. § 4(a).

[3] The Treasury Inspector General for Tax Administration (TIGTA), which was carved out of the Treasury IG and covers a distinct entity within the Treasury Department — the Internal Revenue Service (IRS) — is another comparable, though not identical, IG. TIGTA is currently the only statutory IG that exists within an establishment or entity that also has an agency-wide IG in place.

[4] P.L. 110-343, § 121(b)(2). For comparison, SIGAR is the only presidentially appointed, but not Senate confirmed, IG, while SIGIR is "appointed by the Secretary of Defe nse, in consultation with the Secretary of State." 5 U.S.C. App. § 8G note. However, "[t]he President may appoint the [SIGIR] to serve as the [SIGAR], in which case the [SIGAR] shall have all of the duties, responsibilities, and authorities set forth ... with respect to such appointed position." *Id.*

[5] P.L. 110-343, § 121(b)(3). SIGIR and SIGAR were required to be appointed "not later than 30 days after the date of the enactment" of their respective acts. *See, e.g.*, P.L. 110-181, § 1229(c).

[6] P.L. 110-343, § 121(b)(4).

[7] IG Act, §§ 3(a), 8G(d).

[8] United States Nuclear Regulatory Commission v. Federal Labor Relations Authority, 25 F.3d 229, 235 (4th Cir. 1994).

[9] It is conceivable that the executive branch would raise constitutional objections to the direct reporting requirement for the Inspector General. However, Congress has imposed direct reporting requirements on executive branch officials since the first Congress. CRS Report RL 33667, *Presidential Signing Statements: Constitutional and Institutional Implications*, by T.J. Halstead. Additionally, in *Morrison v. Olson*, 487 U.S. 654 (1988), the Supreme Court established a two-step balancing test for addressing separation of powers concerns in such situations. First, the President must establish that the congressional action interferes with a core power. If so, Congress must show a necessity for its action to overcome the interference. Ultimately, given that removal power remains within the executive branch, the President will be able to perform its constitutional duty to "take care that the laws be faithfully executed." *Morrison*, 487 U.S. at 686, 694-95; U.S. CONST. art. II, § 3. In the IG context, the executive branch would "retain[] ample authority to assure that the [IG] is competently performing his or her statutory responsibilities." Morrison, 487 U.S. at 692.

[10] P.L. 110-343, § 101(a)(3).

[11] IG Act § 8D. If the Treasury Secretary were to exercise this power over the Treasury IG, the Secretary must notify the Treasury IG in writing of the reasons for exercising such power. The Treasury IG, in turn, must send this notification to congressional committees within 30 days.

[12] *See, e.g.*, P.L. 110-181, § 1229(a)(3).

[13] P.L. 110-343, § 104(a)(3). Additionally, the Comptroller General must submit reports on "the activities and performance of the TARP and of any agents or representatives of the TARP" to the SIG TARP at least every 60 days. P.L. 110-343, § 116(a)(3).

[14] 5 U.S.C. §§ 5(a)-(b).

[15] *See, e.g.*, P.L. 110-181, §§ 1229(i)-(k). The President can waive the public availability requirement of the SIGIR and SIGAR reports for national security reasons.

[16] 5 U.S.C. App. § 5(c).

[17] P.L. 110-343, § 116(a)(2)(A).

[18] P.L. 110-181, §§ 1229(h)(4), (6).

[19] *See, e.g.*, P.L. 108-106, § 3001(h)(5).

[20] P.L. 110-343, § 121(h).
[21] P.L. 110-181, § 1221(h), § 1229(o).

INDEX

C

D

E

F

G

H

I

S

T